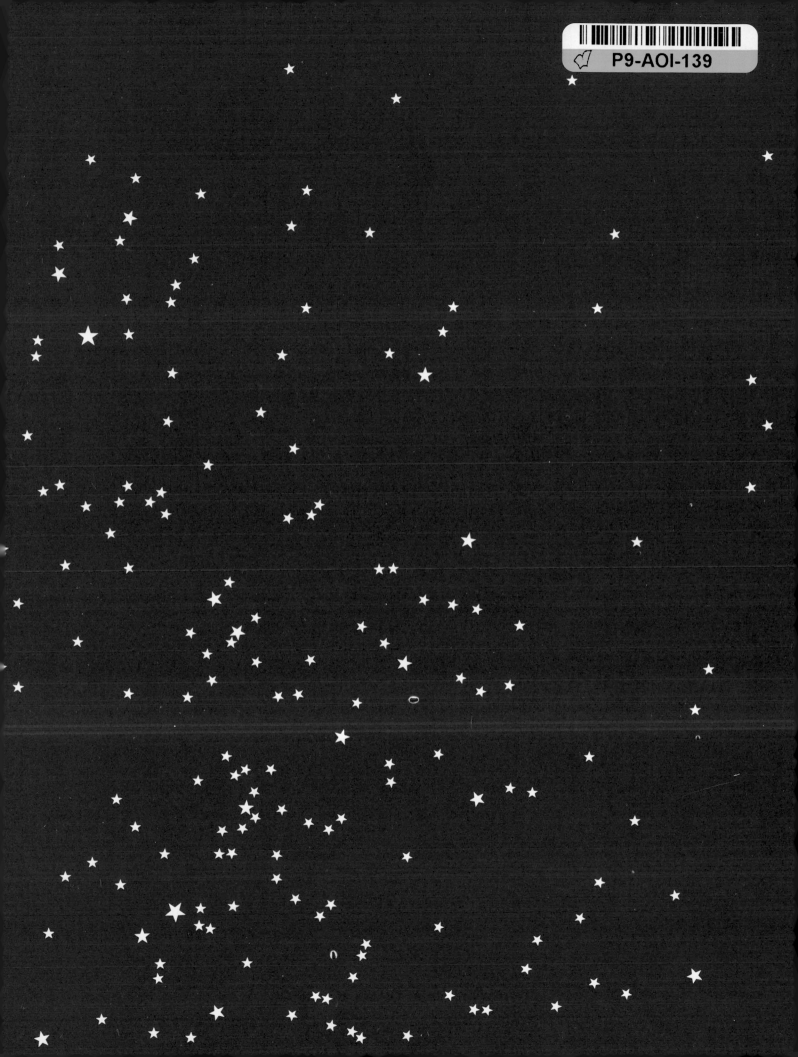

The NOVA Space Explorer's Guide

A NOVA Kids' Book,
Published in association with WGBH Boston,
producers of NOVA for public television

Clarkson N. Potter, Inc. / Publishers   New York
Distributed by Crown Publishers, Inc.

The NOVA
Space Explorer's Guide

Where to Go and What ▓▓▓▓▓
by Richard Maurer

Design by Susan Marsh with Christopher Pullman, WGBH Design

Spacelog

   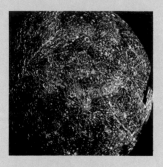

◄

(Front cover) *Astronaut Bruce McCandless rides a jetpack high over planet Earth; note the Space Shuttle reflected in his visor.*

(Opening page) *The Space Shuttle emerges from its "garage"—one of the world's largest buildings.*

(Title page) *Riding a tractor-powered platform, the Shuttle climbs the ramp to the launch pad.*

Published by Clarkson N. Potter, Inc., One Park Avenue, New York, New York 10016 and simultaneously in Canada by General Publishing Company Limited

Manufactured in Hong Kong

Library of Congress Cataloging in Publication Data

Maurer, R. (Richard)
 The nova space explorer's guide.

 1. Outer space—Exploration—Popular
 works. I. Title.
TL793.M38 1985 919.9 84-24905
ISBN 0-517-55752-5

10 9 8 7 6 5 4 3 2 1
First Edition

Acknowledgments: It is a great pleasure to be involved in a project that combines the excitement of exploring space, with the patient search for answers that is the trademark of public television's NOVA science series. For this I thank NASA (the National Aeronautics and Space Administration) and NOVA.

At NASA I have been aided by some half dozen space centers, which are named in the credits on page 118. I am particularly grateful to Mike Gentry at the Johnson Space Center. At NOVA I wish to thank the executive producers, past and present, John Mansfield and Paula Apsell.

Many people work behind the scenes of a book. In this case, the idea of a year ago is now transformed into the object you are holding due to hard work by the staff at WGBH-TV in Boston and Clarkson N.

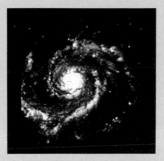
Potter, Publishers in New York. Karen Johnson at WGBH brilliantly managed this enterprise, ably assisted by Carol Hills. Chris Pullman, design and publications manager at WGBH, helped shape the book with inventive (and often amazing) solutions to almost every problem we faced. The original idea was suggested by Carolyn Hart Gavin, senior editor at Clarkson Potter, and she and her colleagues have provided enthusiastic support throughout.

The accuracy of the book owes much to valuable comments from space professionals Jim Head of Brown University and Andy Chaikin of *Sky and Telescope* magazine. The book's drawings are the work of two other professionals, Mary Reilly and Diane McCaffery of Somerville, Massachusetts, who also prepared the pasted-up pages. The type was very handsomely set by DEKR Corporation of Woburn, Massachusetts.

I have dedicated this book, in part, to its designer. I believe more authors should do so, since the designer is the visual author, so to speak. It is the designer who turns a stack of typewritten pages into an honest-to-goodness book. This particular designer has borne more than the usual burdens, since I am married to her. She has commented on my ideas, read through rough drafts, looked at countless photos, and seen a real book behind it the whole time. I cannot imagine the project being completed without her delightful assistance.

This book is also dedicated to my son, Sam. Authors like to imagine an ideal reader, and he is mine—as soon as he learns to read.

Richard Maurer

("T minus six . . . five . . . four") *The pilots of the first Shuttle mission, John Young* (left) *and Bob Crippen* (right), *show thumbs up from behind the controls. Spacesuits were worn for the early test flights.*

("We have main engine start . . .") *Firing room controllers watch as the mighty Shuttle roars to life.*

(Back cover) *Bob Stewart, outfitted for space exploration, hovers outside the window of the Shuttle.*

This book is for Susie and Sam — RM

"We have main engine start..."

"Two...one...zero..."

Chapter 1

Lift-Off!

Everyone knows that the only way to go into space is on a rocket. But why do we want to go? What will we find there?

When you ask people why we send rockets into space, you don't always get the same answer:

"To observe the Earth and learn more about it."

"To bring back Moon rocks."

"To send up satellites for better TV service."

"To look for life on other planets."

There are many reasons to go into space. Some provide obvious benefits. Communications satellites transmit long-distance phone calls. Weather satellites make it possible to predict where storms will strike. Other reasons seem less practical and boil down to simply wanting to go and see what's out there. This is humankind's age-old urge to explore the unknown.

We are about to take off on a trip to explore the great unknown that surrounds us in all directions. It is called the *universe*. Some people say that space is the last frontier. In the chapters ahead we will discover that space is a virtual infinity of frontiers. There are more than a billion billion unknown places out there to explore. This ought to keep us busy for a very long time.

But first things first. Why do we need a rocket for our trip? Why can't we just take an airplane?

Simple enough—an airplane needs air. Not only do an airplane's wings require air for lift, but its engine needs the oxygen in air in order to burn fuel. Down here on the ground it's easy to imagine that the *atmosphere* (which is what scientists call the air) extends forever above our heads. Fish probably assume the same thing about water. In fact, the atmosphere ends about 160 kilometers (100 miles) overhead. One hundred and sixty kilometers is the distance you can drive on the highway

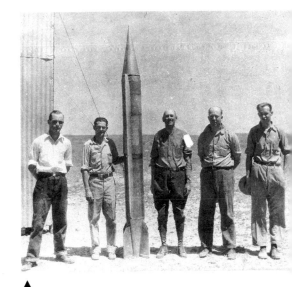

▲
The technology of modern rocketry had its beginnings in the pioneering experiments of Robert Goddard, shown here to the right of one of his test rockets for 1931.

◄
(Opposite) *Anchors aweigh for a Shuttle voyage into space!*

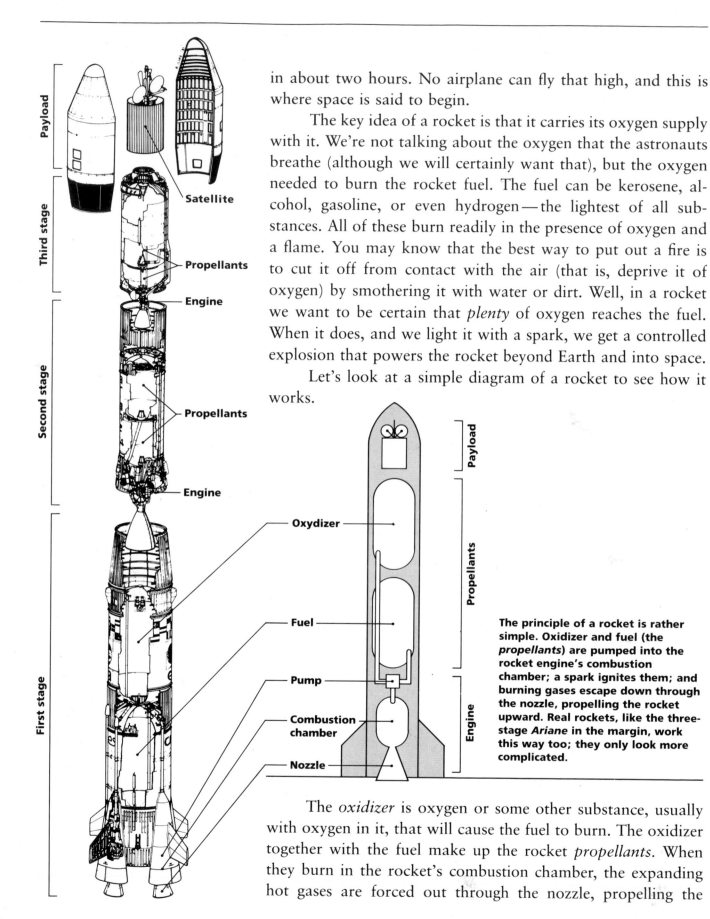

Payload

Satellite

Third stage

Propellants

Engine

Second stage

Propellants

Engine

First stage

in about two hours. No airplane can fly that high, and this is where space is said to begin.

The key idea of a rocket is that it carries its oxygen supply with it. We're not talking about the oxygen that the astronauts breathe (although we will certainly want that), but the oxygen needed to burn the rocket fuel. The fuel can be kerosene, alcohol, gasoline, or even hydrogen—the lightest of all substances. All of these burn readily in the presence of oxygen and a flame. You may know that the best way to put out a fire is to cut it off from contact with the air (that is, deprive it of oxygen) by smothering it with water or dirt. Well, in a rocket we want to be certain that *plenty* of oxygen reaches the fuel. When it does, and we light it with a spark, we get a controlled explosion that powers the rocket beyond Earth and into space.

Let's look at a simple diagram of a rocket to see how it works.

Payload

Propellants

Oxydizer

Fuel

Pump

Combustion chamber

Nozzle

Engine

The principle of a rocket is rather simple. Oxidizer and fuel (the *propellants*) are pumped into the rocket engine's combustion chamber; a spark ignites them; and burning gases escape down through the nozzle, propelling the rocket upward. Real rockets, like the three-stage *Ariane* in the margin, work this way too; they only look more complicated.

The *oxidizer* is oxygen or some other substance, usually with oxygen in it, that will cause the fuel to burn. The oxidizer together with the fuel make up the rocket *propellants*. When they burn in the rocket's combustion chamber, the expanding hot gases are forced out through the nozzle, propelling the rocket upward—or in whichever direction it's pointed.

Notice in the diagram that almost all of the space in a rocket is taken up by the propellant tanks. This is surprising if you consider that this is not true in other kinds of vehicles. Cars and airplanes, for instance, contain mostly passenger and cargo space. It's true that they don't carry their own oxygen with them, but their fuel tanks are still a relatively small part of the vehicle. This tells us that driving a car 160 kilometers (km) on the ground is nothing compared with shooting a rocket 160 km into the air. It takes an enormous amount of fuel to propel a rocket the relatively short distance from Earth into space. For comparison, let's look at the Redstone rocket that carried America's first astronaut, Alan Shepard, 190 km (120 miles) into space. Next to it is a vehicle that takes us about the same distance here on the Earth's surface.

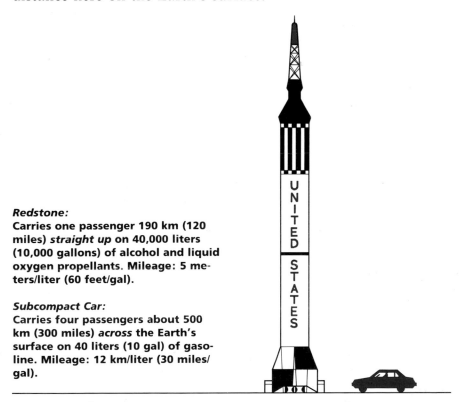

Redstone:
Carries one passenger 190 km (120 miles) *straight up* on 40,000 liters (10,000 gallons) of alcohol and liquid oxygen propellants. Mileage: 5 meters/liter (60 feet/gal).

Subcompact Car:
Carries four passengers about 500 km (300 miles) *across* the Earth's surface on 40 liters (10 gal) of gasoline. Mileage: 12 km/liter (30 miles/gal).

Obviously, rockets are the greatest gas guzzlers of all time! The Redstone uses one thousand times as much stored propellants as a subcompact car, and the Redstone is only a very modest-sized rocket. It was not even capable of putting astronaut Shepard into orbit; his space capsule simply fell back to

The Metric System

The metric system is easy to use, easy to learn, and is the official system of weights and measures among scientists *and* in most of the countries of the world. These are some of the metric units used in this book.

Distance:
- 1 meter (m) = 39 inches (about 1 yard)
- 1 kilometer (km) = 1,000 meters (³⁄₅ of a mile)

Weight:
- 1 gram (gm) = ¹⁄₃₀ of an ounce (about the weight of 2 paper clips)
- 1 kilogram (kg) = 1,000 grams (2¹⁄₅ pounds)

Volume:
- 1 liter (l) = 1¹⁄₁₆ quarts

Temperature:
- 1 degree Centigrade (C) = 1.8 degrees Fahrenheit (The two temperature scales have different starting points. Zero degrees Centigrade is the freezing point of water. Zero degrees Fahrenheit is well below freezing.)

Pluto:
5.8 billion km
3.6 billion miles

Earth:
380,000 km
240,000 miles

Earth's Atmosphere

If you've ever been climbing in the Rocky Mountains, then you know that you don't have to leave the Earth's surface to experience the thinning of the atmosphere. At the elevation of Aspen, Colorado — 2.5 km (1.5 miles) above sea level — people from lower altitudes often feel short of breath after mild exercise.

Mount Everest, the highest point on Earth, reaches to 9 km (5.5 miles), almost four times higher than Aspen. The air on top of Everest is about one-fourth as dense as at sea level. Climbers usually bring their own oxygen with them.

The highest of all clouds are *cirrus.* These wispy veils of ice crystals reach higher than Mount Everest, to about 12 km (7.5 miles). Passenger jets usually fly no higher than this. But some military jets can fly more than twice as high, to 30 km (20 miles). From such heights, pilots can see the curve of the Earth, and the sky is a midnight blue. Are they at the edge of space?

Not yet. In fact, they are only one-fifth of the way there. The atmosphere thins out more and more until, around 160 km (100 miles), it is less than a *trillionth* (a millionth of a millionth) its density at sea level. This is the lowest altitude at which satellites can operate, and it is where space begins.

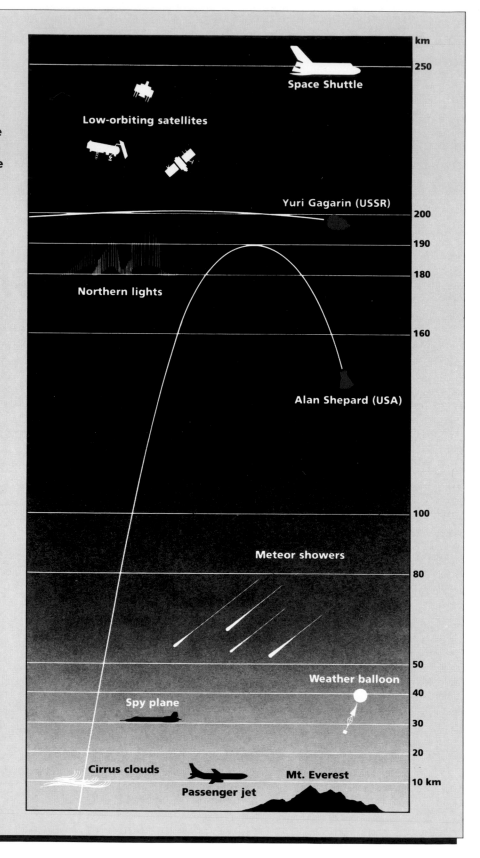

Space Shuttle

Low-orbiting satellites

Yuri Gagarin (USSR)

Northern lights

Alan Shepard (USA)

Meteor showers

Weather balloon

Spy plane

Cirrus clouds

Passenger jet

Mt. Everest

km
250
200
190
180
160
100
80
50
40
30
20
10 km

Earth after a short flight into space. His flight path looked something like this.

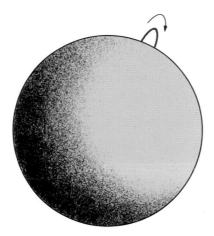

One month before Shepard's flight, on April 12, 1961, the Russian cosmonaut Yuri Gagarin (cosmonaut is what Russians call their space travelers) became the first human in orbit—in fact, the first human in space—flying all the way around the Earth at a maximum altitude of 200 km (125 miles). His flight path looked like this.

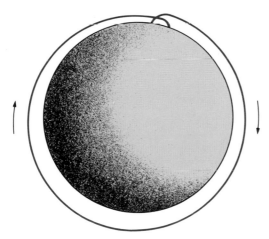

Getting something into orbit takes much more rocket power than just sending it up and then letting it fall back. Once something is going fast enough to get into orbit, it tends to stay there. We will learn more about this in the next chapter.

The flights of Shepard and Gagarin happened over twenty years ago. Now let's see what today's rockets can do. On the next page are a variety of modern rockets. Compare them with the Redstone, which is shown at the same scale. Suddenly, Redstone doesn't look so big.

▲
(Top) *Alan Shepard and his Mercury capsule, safely aboard the recovery ship after a fifteen minute flight into space.*
(Bottom) *Yuri Gagarin, Earth's first space traveler.*

These bigger rockets are more what we had in mind for our trip. Clearly, the bigger the rocket, the more it will carry and the farther it will go. And in the following pages we are planning to go a very long way indeed. Our trip will take us as far as the most distant known planets, Neptune and Pluto— more than 4 billion km (2.5 billion miles) from Earth. Unfortunately, no rocket yet exists that can take human passengers

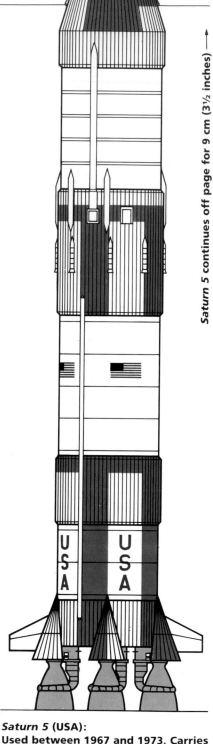

Saturn 5 continues off page for 9 cm (3½ inches) →

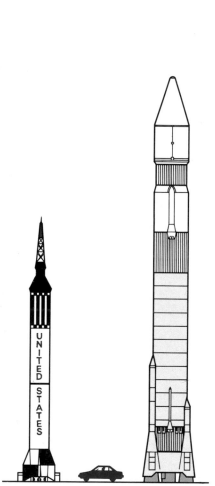

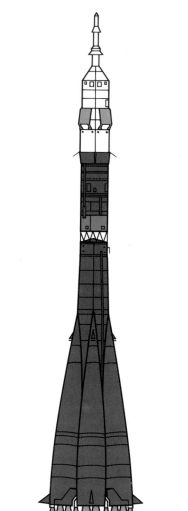

***Atlas-Centaur* (USA):**
First launched in 1966. *Atlas-Centaur*, shown here to the right of Alan Shepard's *Redstone*, can send a cargo of 500 kg (½ ton—about the weight of 30 bicycles) on a voyage of millions of kilometers to the planets. Propellants are kerosene and liquid oxygen in the lower stages, and liquid hydrogen and liquid oxygen in the upper stage. It is not designed to carry passengers.

***Soyuz* (USSR):**
First launched in 1967. Carries 3 passengers—and all of the oxygen, food, and equipment necessary for their survival—into Earth orbit. Propellants are kerosene and liquid oxygen.

***Saturn 5* (USA):**
Used between 1967 and 1973. Carries 3 passengers to the Moon and back (800,000 km, or ½ million miles). Propellants are kerosene and liquid oxygen in the first stage, and liquid hydrogen and liquid oxygen in the second and third stages. This is the largest rocket ever launched.

that far. However, unmanned spaceships with cameras and other instruments are now actually traveling to those remote regions. There is no doubt that astronauts will someday follow.

Our first stop on this journey is Earth orbit, and there is no better way of getting there than the Space Shuttle. So let's climb on board, strap in, check all systems, and take off . . .

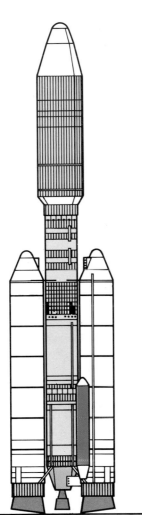

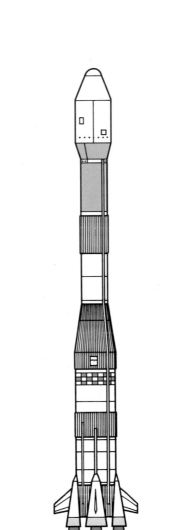

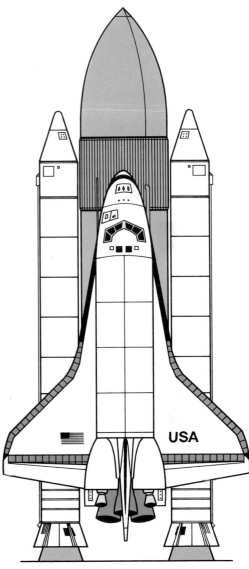

Titan-Centaur (USA):
First launched in 1974. Can send 3,500 kg (4 tons) to Mars or 800 kg (1 ton) on a journey of *billions* of kilometers to Jupiter and beyond. The central section has three stages: the first two use liquid propellants that ignite on contact; the third burns liquid hydrogen and liquid oxygen. There are two solid-propellant strap-on boosters. No passengers.

Ariane (European Space Agency):
First launched in 1979. Can carry up to 4,800 kilograms (5 tons) into Earth orbit. Propellants for the bottom stages are two chemicals that ignite on contact so that no spark is needed. The top stage burns liquid hydrogen and liquid oxygen. No passengers.

Space Shuttle (USA):
First launched in 1981. Carries up to 8 passengers and 30,000 kg (33 tons) of cargo into Earth orbit. Propellants are liquid hydrogen and liquid oxygen, with two strap-on boosters burning solid propellants similar to gunpowder. The Shuttle is the only rocket that can land like an airplane on returning to Earth.

Chapter 2

Space Station Earth

Going . . . going . . . gone! In a matter of minutes we leave the Earth, the clouds and the blue sky behind. As we pick up speed we gradually turn until we are traveling parallel to the ground. At this point the Shuttle is already well into space and moving 16,000 km/hour (10,000 miles/hour). But this is not yet fast enough, for if we were to turn off our engines now we would slowly fall back to Earth.

Around 1665 the young English scientist Isaac Newton had the idea that if an object could be placed above the atmosphere and shot straight ahead with enough force, it would travel around and around the Earth in unending loops. This is just what we're aiming for, and as our engines push us faster and faster, we finally reach 29,000 km/hour (18,000 miles/ hour)—more than thirty times the speed of a passenger jet. After just twelve minutes, we have arrived.

"Control, this is Shuttle. We have achieved orbit."

The rocket engines shut off. We need not keep our engines running now since we will stay in orbit without further propulsion. In space there is almost no friction to slow us down. (There is *some* friction due to almost undetectable amounts of air, even as high as several hundred kilometers. Over time this will cause a spacecraft to fall lower and lower until it re-enters the atmosphere, but this usually takes several years.)

"Roger, Shuttle, this is Control. How's the view up there?"

For the moment our attention is directed *inside*, not outside the ship. Everything is floating!

Everyone has heard about weightlessness in space, but to actually experience it is startling indeed. Imagine that everything not nailed or bolted down in your room is free to float away at the slightest touch. Of course, inside the Shuttle precautions have been taken and practically everything *is* bolted down.

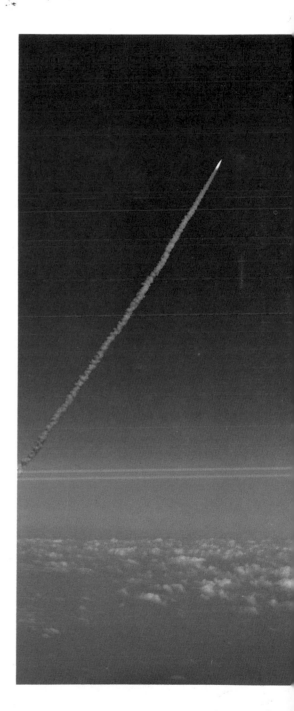

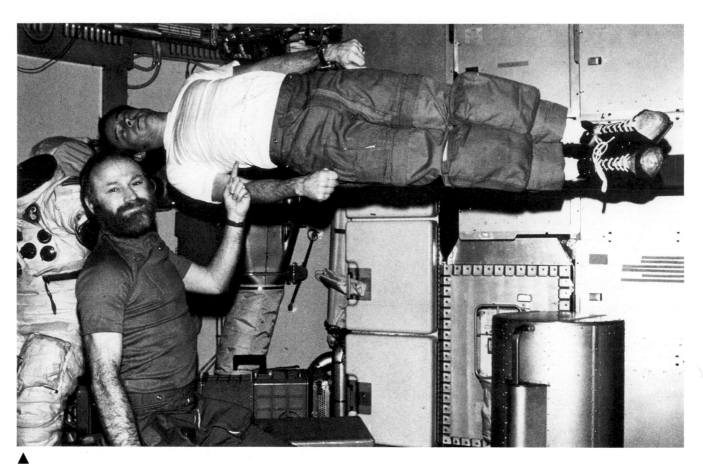

▲
Astronauts aboard the Skylab space station in 1974 demonstrate zero-gravity weightlifting.

▶
(Opposite) Floating underwater is one of the closest Earth experiences to weightlessness. Here a suited-up astronaut trains for a space walk. (Inset) Weightless toothbrushes and toothpaste drift about a medicine cabinet in space.

◀
(Overleaf) Pushed by 3 million kg (3,000 tons) of rocket thrust, the Space Shuttle takes off on a twelve minute trip into orbit.

Nonetheless, many small items that we'd lost track of on the ground—pencils, tape, a flashlight, a pack of gum—have emerged from hiding and are now floating in front of us. The next thing we do is unbuckle so we can float too.

Astronauts say that being weightless is almost like floating underwater. In fact, that is how they train for going into space.

But you can't exactly swim through the air. A frog kick will get you nowhere since you can't push against the air the way you can against water. So getting from one part of the spaceship to another is managed by pushing against the wall, floor, or furniture, sending yourself floating in a straight line until you bump into something. There's a lot of banging around like bumper cars until you get the hang of it. On the other hand, passing your fellow astronaut the ketchup is as simple as giving the bottle a little push in his or her direction, where it gently arrives after a slow, graceful flight. Getting the ketchup out of the bottle is another matter. (We'll solve that problem a little later.)

Life Aboard the Shuttle: The Cabin

The Space Shuttle is America's space truck. It can carry several satellites into orbit, drop them off and then return to Earth, landing like an airplane. (The Shuttle's two booster rockets and the giant fuel tank—shown in the drawing on page 7—don't actually go into orbit; they are discarded on the way up.)

As in any truck, the passenger cabin is relatively small. Most of the vehicle is taken up by cargo space. Even so, the Shuttle cabin is designed to carry up to eight people, and keep them well fed, rested, and busy about their duties for a week or more. The cabin has about as much interior space as a very small mobile home, or a camper-trailer. There are two levels: an upper deck where all the flight controls (and most of the windows) are; and a lower deck where the sleeping bunks, storage lockers, food galley, and washroom are located.

Once you are in orbit and weightless, the tiny area seems to expand. Every surface—walls, floor, and ceiling—becomes usable space as you float about with the freedom of a fish in water.

(Top) *The Shuttle cargo bay open, with the mechanical arm extended.* (Right) *Astronaut Sally Ride asleep in a sleep restraint.*

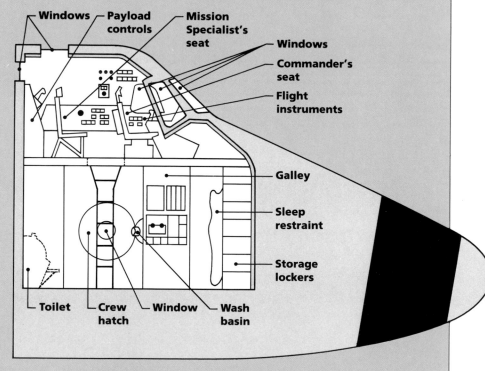

Windows — Payload controls — Mission Specialist's seat — Windows — Commander's seat — Flight instruments — Galley — Sleep restraint — Storage lockers — Toilet — Crew hatch — Window — Wash basin

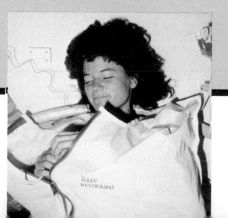

Isaac Newton

Isaac Newton (1642–1727) is famous for discovering the theory of universal gravitation upon seeing an apple drop to the ground. How could a falling apple make anyone think of something so complicated? It simply occurred to Newton that the force that pulls an apple toward the Earth, and keeps us stuck securely in our chairs, *also* pulls on the distant Moon. He extended this idea to show that the Sun's gravity is responsible for the orbital motion of the Earth and the other planets. Indeed, Newton showed that all objects in the universe, no matter how large or small, attract each other with a gravitational force that depends on the mass (weight) of the objects, and the distance between them.

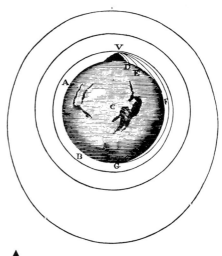

▲
A drawing from Newton's book showing that a cannonball shot from a high mountain travels farther and farther (to distances D, E, F, and G), the faster it is projected. Newton realized that the cannonball could be made to travel completely around the Earth—the very principle of an orbiting satellite.

You may wonder what causes this delightful condition. Weightlessness, as the word implies, is a state where objects have no apparent weight. We are all familiar with weight. It is the measurement you get when you place an object on a scale. What you are actually measuring is the force of gravity pulling the object toward the center of the Earth.

Suppose that you were standing on a scale and the floor suddenly gave in—dropping you to a mattress factory in the basement, let's say. On your way down the scale would read zero, even with your feet touching it. The fact that both you and the scale were falling would make you (and it) momentarily weightless.

Believe it or not, this is exactly the situation on our orbiting Shuttle. The Earth is continually tugging at the Shuttle, pulling it in a curved path—a perpetual fall—around and around the globe. Because we and everything on board are falling with the Shuttle—and falling at the same rate—you may stick out your hand and "drop" something, but it's not going to go anywhere, since it's already falling as fast as it can.

Life Aboard the Shuttle: Food and Drink

If you like peanut butter, graham crackers, pecan cookies, almond crunch bars, nuts, hard candy, and gum, you're in luck! These are about the only foods aboard the Shuttle that come in their natural forms. Everything else is dehydrated, freeze dried, canned, or irradiated (sterilized with radiation) — but that's not to say it isn't delicious. Consider the menu for your first evening in space:

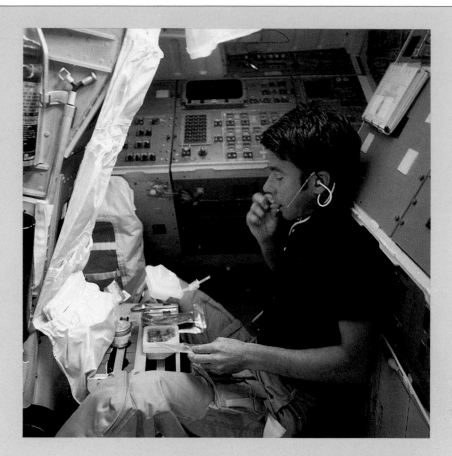

APPETIZER
shrimp cocktail

MAIN COURSE
beefsteak with gravy

VEGETABLES
broccoli au gratin
rice pilaf

SALAD
fruit cocktail

DESSERT
chocolate pudding

BEVERAGE
coffee, tea, or fruit juice

Not bad, even if you do have to eat out of plastic containers. All that's missing is candlelight and soft music!

(Top) Astronaut Lenoir enjoys (?) a bite of space food, while his beverage floats conveniently above his tray. (Right) A reconstituted "cup" of coffee.

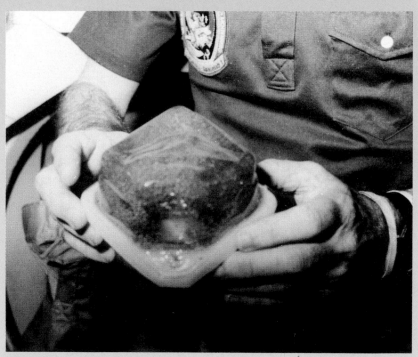

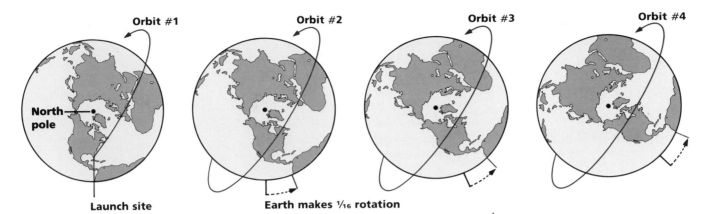

Orbit #1   Orbit #2   Orbit #3   Orbit #4

North pole

Launch site   Earth makes ¹⁄₁₆ rotation

While the Shuttle circles the Earth in a fixed orbit, the Earth turns beneath it. In this drawing, we are looking down on the north pole as the Shuttle orbits once every ninety minutes. Earth makes one-sixteenth rotation during each orbit. Notice how each new orbit takes the Shuttle over a different part of the globe.

So it will appear to just float. Everything on board will float because everything is falling.

Before you lose your breath thinking about this, let's look out the window.

"Shuttle, this is Control. You should be passing over Norway about now."

"It's beautiful—fantastic! Those glaciers make it look mighty cold down there."

"Roger, and in three minutes you'll be over Moscow."

The ground flies by at quite a rate up here. In just an hour and a half we will have completed our first orbit. This is a far cry from the three years that it took Magellan's sailing ships on the first trip around the world in the 1500s. Later in the book we will find that three years nowadays will take us as far as the planet Saturn.

Soon we're within sight of India. Then we cross the Indian Ocean just missing Australia, and fly up the southern Pacific passing over North America considerably west of our launch site.

The Earth has made a one-sixteenth turn in its daily rotation since our launch ninety minutes ago, and our next orbit will take us several thousand kilometers to the west of our first. Our third orbit will be several thousand kilometers west of that, and so on, until, after sixteen orbits (twenty-four hours), the Earth has made one complete revolution beneath us.

Space is surely the perfect place to watch the world go by. Up here our school geography lessons are as clear as the view out the window. Mountain ranges, rivers, storms, volcanoes, glaciers, and lots and lots of ocean—all pass beneath us in time.

Life Aboard the Shuttle: Suiting Up

The days are long gone when astronauts lumbered to their launch rocket in bulky space suits. Nowadays passengers on the Space Shuttle take off in a shirtsleeve environment.

No one puts on a space suit unless they're going outside —into space.

Suiting-up is also a lot easier than in the old days. Getting into one of the old suits required up to an hour, and the assistance of another person. The new Shuttle space suit takes one person five minutes to put on, as demonstrated here.

0 min.

1 min.

2 min.

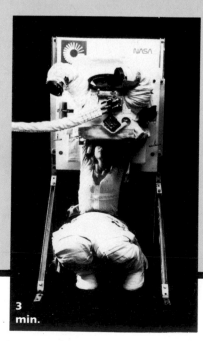

3 min.

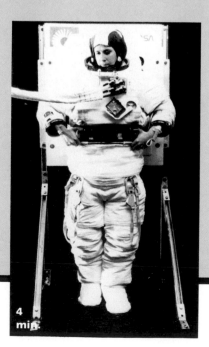

4 min.

5 min.

Variety is really the Earth's claim to fame, and seeing so many different features in so short a time may cause you to wonder how they all fit together in the great puzzle of our planet. How do we make sense of all this variety? What does it tell us? These are the questions explorers naturally ask.

The first thing we do is try to give the simplest possible answer. Clearly, the Earth's surface seems to be made up of land and water. Scientists call the land the *lithosphere* (from *lithos,* the ancient Greek word for stone). The watery part they call the *hydrosphere* (from the Greek word *hudor,* meaning water).

The land and the water are the first things we notice about Earth. But on closer inspection we notice something else. If we look at the Earth's *limb*—the round edge where the planet is outlined against space—then we can see a very thin haze wrapping the surface.

This is another kind of ocean—the "ocean of air"—which is, of course, the atmosphere (*atmos* in Greek means vapor). And out here in space where we have to carry our own air supply on the ship, we know how important that insubstantial-looking film of air is.

▼

A sunset seen from space shows the Earth's atmosphere up to about 30 km (20 miles). The atmosphere reddens as it grows denser closer to the surface. Below about 10 km (6 miles) silhouetted cloud shapes begin to appear. Compare the different levels to the drawing on page 4.

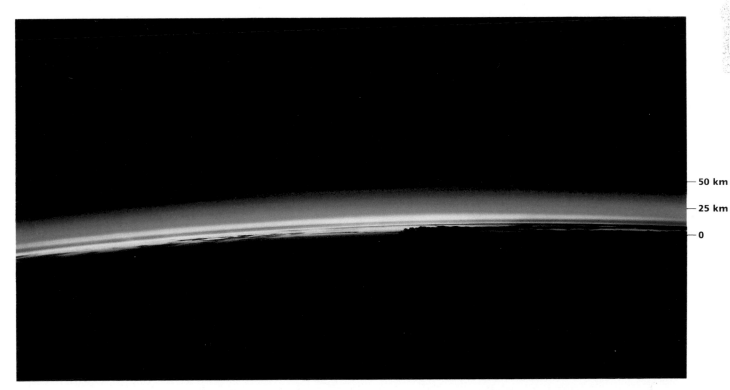

—50 km

—25 km

—0

Earth

- **Position:**
  Third planet from the Sun

- **Distance from Sun:**
  150 million km
  (93 million miles)

- **Length of year:**
  365.26 days

- **Length of day:**
  24 hours

- **Diameter:**
  12,800 km (8,000 miles)

The Earth spins once on its axis in 24 hours and makes a complete orbit of the Sun in slightly over 365 days. These familiar numbers are of course our day and year. No doubt their lengths seem just about right to us. But as we visit other planets we will find that days and years elsewhere have very different, and often peculiar, values.

Earth   Texas

1200 km

▶

The highest mountains on Earth, photographed from 240 km (150 miles) in space. Mount Everest is circled. (Opposite) Close-up of a remote Himalayan region along the Indian-Tibetan border.

Lithosphere, hydrosphere, and atmosphere. In order to understand more about them, let's look at some specific examples as seen out of our Shuttle window.

"Shuttle, this is Control. For the next two minutes you'll be over the Tibetan Plateau."

Coming into view are the Himalayan mountains in Tibet —the highest mountains in the world. They are clearly part of the continent of Asia, which is part of the lithosphere. But is it as simple as that? Well, look a little closer, because there is snow on those mountains. The snow falls on the mountaintops, melts and runs down into the valleys where it collects into rivers, and the rivers run to low points where the water collects into lakes. All of these processes are visible in the picture on the opposite page.

The water, as we have seen, is the Earth's hydrosphere. And this is not just the oceans, but the snow, rivers, lakes, and glaciers as well. Where did the snow come from in the first place? Water vapor in the atmosphere condensed into clouds and then froze as ice crystals which fell to Earth. And so in this scene we have the interaction of all three "spheres" on our planet.

Mt. Everest

You are here

100 km

▲
The Grand Canyon snakes across northern Arizona in a satellite view from space, and (top) in a close-up from the canyon's south rim. The satellite picture shows where the photographer of the top photo was standing, and shows the view taken in by his camera.

▶
A hurricane—Earth's most fearsome storm.

Let's look at another example.

Three orbits later we pass over the famous Grand Canyon in Arizona.

Seen from space, the canyon shows up as rough country on either side of the jagged Colorado River. Perhaps you have been to the Grand Canyon and have seen its spectacular scenery from the ground. There is no question why it is called "grand." There is also no question that this enormous chasm was dug by the erosive action of the Colorado River. Our view from space shows this erosion dramatically. Over time the river has cut, caved in, and washed away the land on either side of it. This is another example of how the lithosphere is shaped by forces of the hydrosphere.

And what of the atmosphere? As we have seen, it is involved in this process to the extent that rivers are fed by rain and snow that falls from the sky. But the atmosphere can act with spectacular forces too. Chief among these is the hurricane—one of which we see at the right as we pass over the Gulf of Mexico.

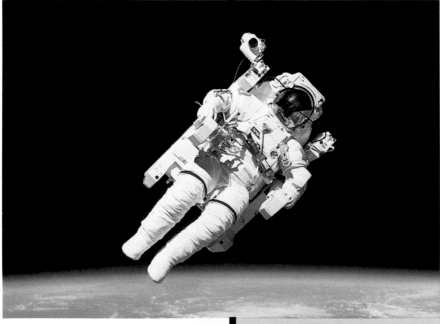

A "Walk" in Space

If you like the view from inside a spaceship, wait until you go outside. "If you stand outdoors," says one astronaut, "it's like being on the front end of a locomotive as it's going down the track! But there's no noise, no vibration; everything's silent and motionless."

Several dozen men and women have ventured outdoors on "spacewalks" to make repairs, clean windows, change film, and do other chores. But they need "walk" no more. In the old days they grappled with hand- and footholds while a coil of safety cord kept them from drifting away if they lost their grip. Nowadays, astronauts can put on a jetpack and zoom away to a nearby satellite; they can hover for hours over a tricky repair job, or direct space traffic. As it sounds, the jetpack is a jet-powered backpack with twenty-four tiny nozzles shooting out compressed gas for propulsion.

The jetpack will be an important tool in the future development of space. When space construction projects get started, the on-site supervisor will no doubt wear one. And if a space rescue is ever necessary, an astronaut with a jetpack will probably save the day.

(Top) *Ed White on America's first space walk in 1965.* (Left) *Bruce McCandless tests the first jetpack nineteen years later.*

Hurricanes are the greatest storms on Earth. Their winds can reach 300 km/hour (200 miles/hour), and a typical storm will cover an area the size of Texas. Because hurricanes feed on moist air rising from tropical oceans, they are a good example of the close interaction of the hydrosphere and atmosphere. Of course, when a hurricane strikes land its violent winds and rain begin to affect the lithosphere as well.

We are beginning to see how the three most distinctive features of our planet—the land, the water, and the air—depend on and influence each other to create the familiar face of planet Earth. Let's look at another example. This time it shows how the land has a surprising effect on the air.

In time our orbit takes us over the islands of Indonesia, just northwest of Australia. As we look down and scan the scene, we see a very interesting sight.

"Shuttle to Control. I believe we've spotted an erupting volcano down there."

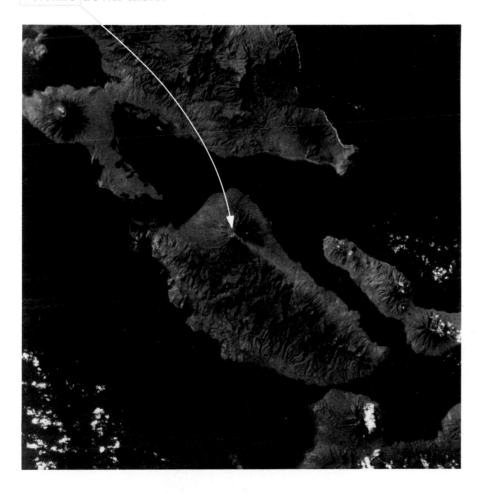

◄
A volcano on Adonara Island in Indonesia trails a plume of smoke 50 km (30 miles) long.

And indeed we have. It looks like a tiny mountain on fire. Actually, the volcano is pouring smoke and fire from the very insides of the Earth. Over the several billion years of Earth's history, many such volcanoes have spewed smoke, fire, and huge amounts of gas and water vapor into the air. In fact, they were *creating* the air, because this is where the atmosphere came from. It came out of the Earth itself—from gases escaping from molten lava.

Things have quieted down since then, but even today there are always a few volcanoes active somewhere on Earth. This connection between volcanoes and the atmosphere is something we will keep in mind as we head out to explore the other planets. We will also keep an eye out for other Earthlike features that we can find, for when you go traveling you always compare the new sights with home.

As we get ready to leave Earth orbit and head out into

▼
An oasis of life in the sandy desert. Farmlands created by irrigation show up as a patchwork of red and yellow in this view of the Colorado River Delta in arid northern Mexico near the U.S. border. Vegetation appears in false colors because of special detectors used by the satellite.

▼
The oceans harbor many lifeforms. Here we can see aqua-colored reefs built-up over centuries by living coral.

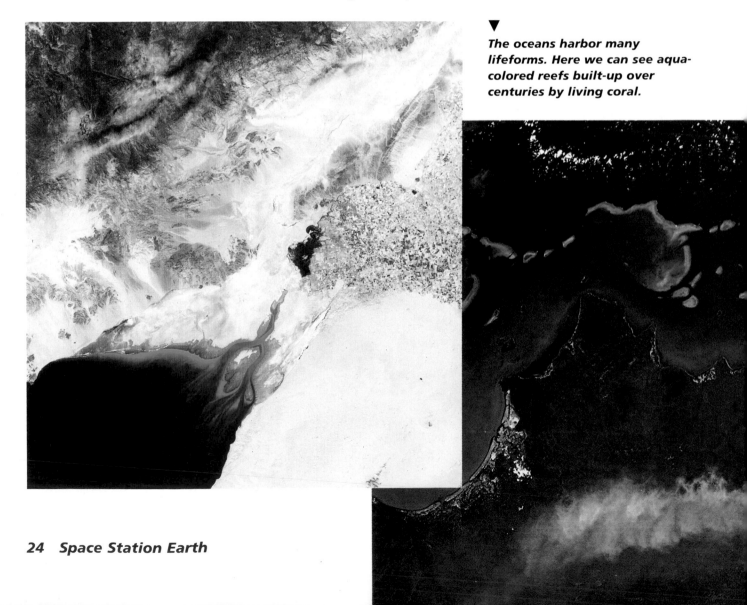

deep space, we think we have pretty much seen the sights on our home planet. We have studied the lithosphere, hydrosphere, and atmosphere—the great systems that interact to make Earth the fascinating place that it is.

Could we have left something out? After all, why is the rain important? Or the oceans? And what makes the air so necessary? Or a field of wet earth at all interesting?

It is, of course, life itself that depends on these things: the plants that grow in the earth, the animals that breathe the air, the fish that live in the water. From space you can detect evidence of life almost everywhere—in the irrigated fields of the desert Southwest, the living reefs of coral off the Australian coast, or the cities along the shores of the Great Lakes.

This teeming life that exists in the fragile balance of earth, air, and water makes up the fourth great "sphere" on our planet—the *biosphere* (*bios* is the Greek word for life). From

▼
From space, human society shows up in our cities. Below are Detroit and Toledo, two ports on Lake Erie. They appear as blue-gray networks of concrete and asphalt, because cities are mostly streets. Red is used by the satellite to indicate vegetation, which flourishes in this July scene.

▼
The smoke on land is also a sign of life. It comes from grass fires set to clear pasture land for cattle.

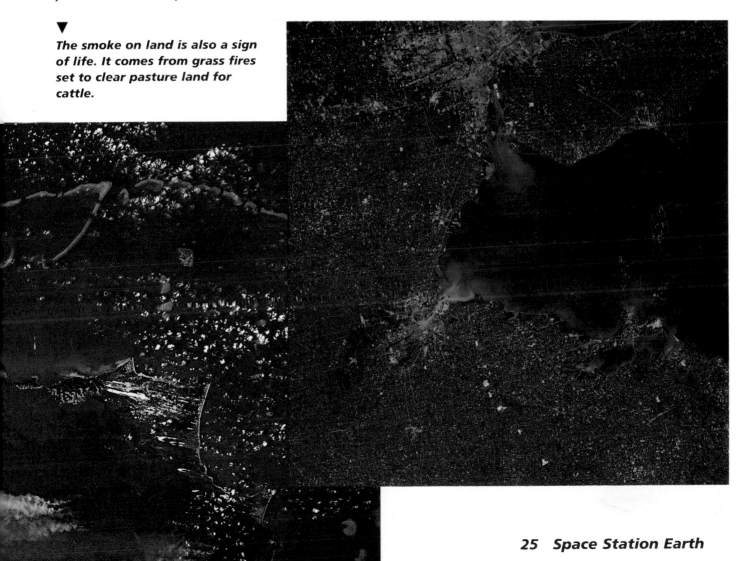

Return to Earth

When the time comes to return to Earth, the pilot of the Space Shuttle fires a pair of braking rockets for three minutes, dropping the ship back into the atmosphere. Still traveling 27,000 km/hour (17,000 miles/hour), the Shuttle must slow down by 99 percent in order to land safely. How does it do this? The air actually does the work, resisting the speeding space plane, slowing it and at the same time heating it to a fiery red.

The hottest part of re-entry lasts about twelve minutes. Then the Shuttle must glide for 900 km (600 miles), slowing itself still more until it reaches the ground at 350 km/hour (220 miles/hour) squarely on top of a runway 90 meters (300 feet) wide. Returning to Earth is every bit as thrilling as leaving it.

▲
Astronaut Crippen pilots the Shuttle back into the atmosphere, as air friction floods the windows with an eerie orange glow.

our human perspective it almost seems that the lithosphere, hydrosphere, and atmosphere exist so that we—the biosphere—can exist. It is as if Earth were an enormous self-supporting space station that supplies us and our fellow creatures with the food, water, and air we need to survive. Space Station Earth supplies us with the materials to build our cities, factories, farms, roads, and automobiles. And it supplies us with the materials to build spaceships . . . so that, if we like, we can leave.

In order to leave Earth orbit we must accelerate our ship to 39,000 km/hour (24,000 miles/hour). The Shuttle can't reach that speed, but if we imagine that we're aboard the Apollo lunar spaceship, powered by the upper stage of the *Saturn 5*, then we will be able to take off for our nearest neighbor—the Moon.

"Prepare for translunar rocket burn in ten seconds . . . nine . . . eight . . . seven . . ."

▶
Earth's nearest neighbor beckons through the window of a spaceship in Earth orbit.

1,000 km from Earth

20,000 km from Earth

Chapter 3

To the Moon

As we watch the Earth getting ever smaller in our window, we can almost imagine how Columbus and his crew felt as they watched Europe disappear over the horizon. Unlike Columbus, though, we can keep our destination in constant view. We're sailing for the Moon!

Columbus sailed for more than two months before reaching America, but our destination is only three days away. Of course, our speed is far greater than that of the *Niña, Pinta,* and *Santa Maria,* so, while we are going some sixty times farther than Columbus, we are also going a *thousand* times faster. If Columbus had been able to sail the ocean of space in his slow-moving ships, it would have taken him ten years to reach the Moon.

340,000 km from Earth
10,000 km to the Moon

▲
Approaching Earth's moon

30,000 km from Earth

◀
(Opposite and left) *Earth rapidly recedes over the course of an hour as three astronauts head for their target, seen above. Note North America in the photo from 20,000 km; and Africa, Arabia, and Antarctica in the scene from 30,000 km.*

To the Moon and Back

Going to the Moon on one of the Apollo expeditions meant departing Earth at the top of a rocket taller than the Statue of Liberty, and then returning in a tiny vehicle the size of an automobile. Along the way there were many steps as various pieces of the mighty rocketship were discarded.

To the Moon . . .

1 *Saturn 5* lifts off
2 Second stage fires
3 Third stage fires
4 Earth orbit
5 Leave for Moon
6 Command-service module turns to dock with lunar module; third stage separates
7 Midcourse correction (if needed)
8 In lunar orbit; lunar module separates
9 Command module stays in orbit
10 Lunar module descent rocket fires
11 Touchdown!

. . . and Back

12 Lift-off, leaving descent stage behind
13 Rendezvous with command module
14 Docking and crew transfer
15 Lunar module discarded
16 Midcourse correction (if needed)
17 Command module separates from service module
18 Command module turns so heat shield faces forward; re-enter Earth's atmosphere
19 Chutes deploy
20 Splashdown in the ocean

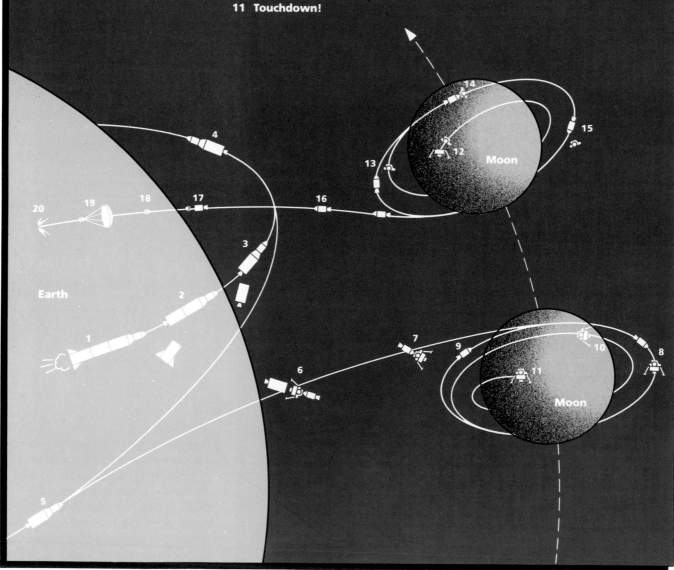

Between 1968 and 1972 the United States launched nine Apollo lunar expeditions. Six of these actually landed men on the Moon's surface. The other three circled the Moon without landing. So far, these have been the only manned voyages to another world. Five hundred years from now, people will probably think of these trips in the same way we think of Columbus's, five hundred years before our own time. Perhaps the Apollo trips will seem dangerous and primitive. They will certainly be remembered as pioneering.

Since we are aboard an Apollo spaceship, let's see just what kind of vehicle it is. Here is how it looks as it cruises toward the Moon.

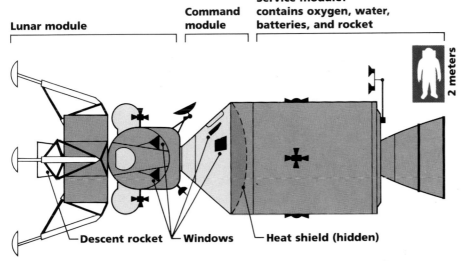

Lunar module   Command module   Service module: contains oxygen, water, batteries, and rocket

2 meters

Descent rocket   Windows   Heat shield (hidden)

The command module is the sleek cone-shaped piece in the middle. On the inside it is about as roomy as a station wagon and it is home to three astronauts during the entire voyage. It is also the only part of the Apollo spaceship that returns to Earth. This is because it has a heat shield for protection during the fiery re-entry into Earth's atmosphere, when the rush of air against the spaceship produces extremely high temperatures. The heat shield is not built onto the other parts of Apollo.

When we get close enough to the Moon we will want to go down and see what it's like on the surface. For that purpose we have a special vehicle — the lunar module. It is the spidery machine attached to the front of the command module. No heat shield is required for landing on the Moon for reasons we will soon discover.

The Moon

- **Position:**
  In orbit around Earth

- **Distance from Earth:**
  380,000 km (240,000 miles)

- **Period of orbit:**
  27.3 Earth days (about one month)

- **Length of day:**
  27.3 Earth days

- **Diameter:**
  3,500 km (2,160 miles — ¼ Earth's diameter)

It's no coincidence that the Moon takes about a month to orbit the Earth. The word "month" comes from the Old English word for Moon. Almost all cultures began keeping time by noting the regular four week cycle of the Moon's changing appearance. (Note that the lunar day also lasts a month!)

Earth   Moon

20,000 km to the Moon

▲
At this point the astronauts can begin to see the portion of the Moon that is invisible from Earth. The "backside" begins just to the right of the dark central spot.

▼
(Below) *Astronaut Cunningham makes observations through the command module window on* **Apollo 7. (Right)** *Buzz Aldrin, in the* **Apollo 11** *lunar module, talks to Earth.*

In order to get down to the Moon, two astronauts climb into the lunar module through a tunnel that connects it with the command module. They then detach their vehicle and descend to the Moon's surface, landing upright on the module's spindly legs. The command module stays behind in lunar orbit, tended by the third astronaut. When Columbus set foot on the shores of America, he arrived in a rowboat that had been launched from his flagship, the *Santa Maria*. In similar fashion our astronauts arrive on the Moon in their lunar "rowboat," while the mother ship waits in deeper water. But we're getting ahead of our story, since our Apollo ship is still many thousands of kilometers from the Moon.

What do astronauts do for three days while they're traveling between Earth and the Moon?

They chart their course.

They talk with Ground Control.

They try to keep clean. (Try it in a station wagon.)

And they eat breakfast, lunch, and dinner.

In the last chapter we talked about the strange effects of weightlessness. Imagine what it's like to eat in space! Here on Earth we trust our food to stay on the plate while we're trying to eat it. No such luck in space. Peas go scattering like marbles. Your hamburger slips out from the bun and floats away. Potato chips emit a cloud of crumbs with every bite.

To make mealtime less hectic, our space meals come pack-

aged in little plastic bags. Macaroni and cheese for lunch? Take out the freeze-dried package. Attach the water injector and give a couple of squirts of warm water. Knead well. Snip off a corner and enjoy.

Perhaps you prefer your macaroni and cheese with ketchup? Take out the squeeze bottle of ketchup and squirt some in. Aboard our spaceship most liquids come in these squeeze bottles, since there is no way to pour anything without the aid of gravity. Try it and you will be chasing little quivering spheres of liquid all over the cabin.

After lunch we tidy up and do some chores. We checked our course earlier and noticed that we'd wandered off a bit. So we briefly fire up one of our rockets to get us back on track. This interplanetary navigation is a complicated business and we must constantly check our position with the stars and with the radar controllers back on Earth, who can follow our progress with the aid of giant radar antennas.

We are not aiming right smack at the Moon but just to one side of it. The plan is that as we fly past we will turn the spaceship so that the big command module engine is facing the direction we are moving. Then we will fire it up to brake our speed. This is exactly the reverse of what we did in the last chapter to leave Earth orbit. By slowing down we will again enter orbit, but this time around the Moon! A check out the window tells us we should get ready soon.

▲
Tracking antennas such as this one were critical in guiding the Apollo missions to the Moon and back.

▼
(Left) Jack Schmitt shaves aboard Apollo 17, while his colleague Ron Evans (below) *has a drink from a zero-gravity squeeze bottle.*

2,000 km to the Moon

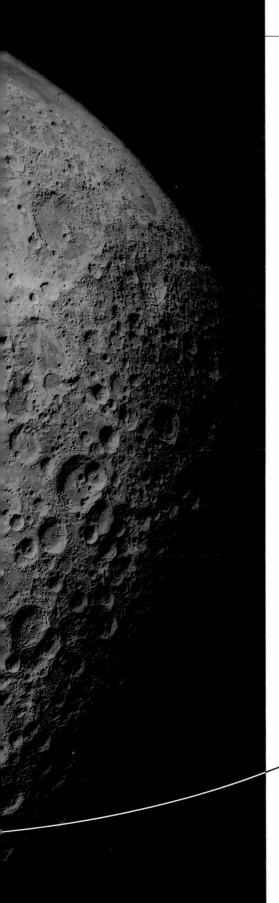

"The most awesome sphere I have ever seen," is how astronaut Mike Collins described the Moon as he guided Apollo 11 into lunar orbit in 1969. (These two views are from Apollo 16, three years later.) The closer astronauts got, the more battered and beat-up the Moon looked. The crater below is clearly one of the smaller ones, yet it is 80 km (50 miles) wide, and 4 km (2.5 miles) deep. All of New York City, its harbor, and many of its suburbs would fit neatly inside; and nine Empire State Buildings, stacked one atop the other, would reach from the crater floor to the rim. The mast jutting from the right edge of the picture holds one of Apollo's scientific instruments.

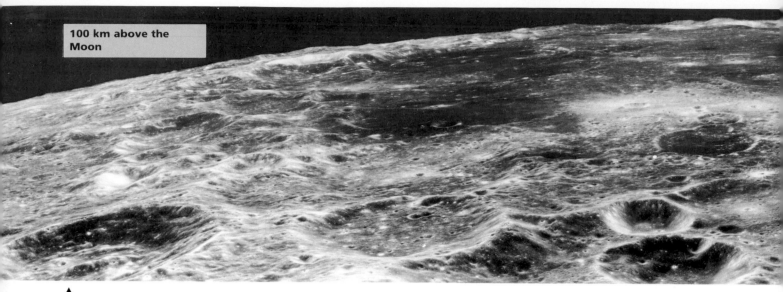

100 km above the Moon

▲

The view from lunar orbit.

"Apollo, this is Control. Prepare for lunar orbit insertion."

We strap into our couches, being careful to also strap down any floating objects since they will become dangerous projectiles when we light our engines. Then we get the spacecraft turned around and fire up our rocket for six minutes. This slows our velocity to about 3,000 km/hour (2,000 miles/hour) and allows the Moon's gravitational field to capture our little spaceship. Instead of flying past the Moon we are now serenely circling it. This "braking maneuver" is a trick we will try in Chapter 5 to get into orbit around Mars.

Our trip out has prepared us to think that the Moon may be a little different from Earth. After all, the Moon's pale yellow scarcely matches the Earth's sparkling blue and white. But a look out the window tells us that this place is *totally* different.

It is a battered, desolate landscape. The nearest we have seen to this is the Himalayan mountains back on Earth. But in the cratered wasteland below there are no cool snows or clear blue lakes. There are no rivers or oceans. There seems to be no water at all, not even clouds—just battered hills and mountains.

The fact that there are no clouds is a clue that we should think about. If you recall from the last chapter, clouds are condensations of water vapor in the air—an interaction between the hydrosphere and atmosphere. Could it be that the absence of clouds, besides signifying that there is no water, might also mean that there is *no air*?

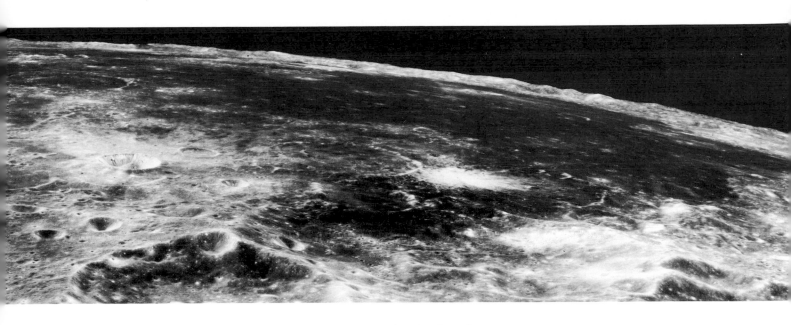

The best way to check this is to look at the limb where the surface seems to touch the inky black of space. When we looked at the Earth's limb in the last chapter, we saw a shimmering layer of air hugging the surface and extending many kilometers into space. This is, of course, our familiar and comforting atmosphere. A look at the Moon's limb shows us no such welcoming sign.

◄

Apollo's geochemical probe points at the Moon's sharply outlined limb. There is no sign of an atmosphere. Compare with the photo of Earth's limb on page 17.

37 To the Moon

No water. No air. The only consolation is that with no air to heat up the outside of our lunar module we will not need a heat shield in order to land. On the other hand, we will not be able to just stroll out onto the surface and take a deep breath, either. We will have to wear space suits, because on the Moon space extends down to the very surface.

Our first look at the Moon has told us that there is neither water nor air, just a pockmarked landscape of craters. There are even craters on top of the craters . . . and craters on top of those. The main feature of the Moon seems to be craters. This is another reason why the Moon looks so different from Earth. There are practically no craters at all on Earth. There are a few, but let's see just how puny they are by Moon standards. On the bottom of the next page is a typical 6,000-square-km (2,300-square-mile) region of the Moon—an area slightly larger than the state of Delaware.

If you have some free time you can probably count several hundred craters of all sizes in this picture. If you were on the Moon's surface you could count millions! Below is a same-sized region of the Earth's surface—notable because it has one of Earth's best-preserved craters on it. (You will also find typical Earth features such as mountains, snow, rivers, and highways.)

Do you see the crater? Hard to spot, isn't it? At the left we see how it looks from an airplane. This one-kilometer-wide hole in the ground was formed about 25,000 years ago when a meteor crashed into our planet.

▼
(Below) *The most impressive crater on Earth is seen from an airplane, and* **(right)** *from space.*

Earth

It's very impressive out in the middle of a flat plain on Earth, but on the Moon we would hardly notice it. Why is it that the Moon, our close neighbor in space, has so many more craters than Earth? We'll try to answer that question a little later in the book after we've seen some of the other planets.

Meanwhile, our curiosity has been aroused during our tour from lunar orbit. Now it's time to go down to the surface for a closer look.

We have done some scouting around for interesting landing sites and have decided to set down next to a winding lunar canyon known as Hadley Rille. (*Apollo 15* actually landed here in July 1971 with astronauts Dave Scott and Jim Irwin.) On Earth, canyons like this are formed by running water. On the bone-dry Moon, they seem oddly out of place.

Could this canyon have been formed long ago by a lunar river? Did the Moon once have water? We will soon see.

Two of us climb aboard the lunar module and set off, leaving our fellow astronaut, who must stay behind in the command module.

"Bon voyage, Columbus," he says over the radio. "Bring back lots of those Moon rocks." We should be seeing him again, with our load of rocks, after a three-day stay on the surface.

"Hold the fort," we call back.

Just as we slowed down the Apollo spaceship to allow the Moon to capture us in orbit, we must now slow ourselves still further if we want to make it down to the surface. So we step

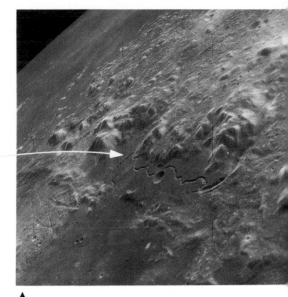

▲

Hadley Rille, our target on the Moon, weaves its way along a chain of lunar mountains. Soon we will see how this scenery looks from the ground.

Moon

◄

This view from lunar orbit shows a region identical in size to the satellite picture of Earth on the opposite page. Clearly, craters are a serious fact of life on the Moon.

39   To the Moon

▲

An astronaut packs up the moon buggy for an unearthly drive. The tracks lead back to the Apollo lunar module. In the distance are mountains as tall as the Rockies. (They are visible from orbit in the photo at the top of page 39.)

▶

(Opposite) The V-shaped canyon, Hadley Rille—1.5 km (1 mile) wide and 300 m (1,000 feet) deep. Not a trickle of water.

on the brakes, firing the lunar module descent rocket to bring us below the Moon's orbital velocity. With our engine firing all the way, we gradually drop toward the surface.

"OK, Control, we're 300 feet over the Moon now, descending at 6 feet per second. Two hundred feet now . . . 150 . . . down at 3 feet per second. We can see our shadow . . . 75 feet, kicking up some dust . . . 30 . . . 10 . . . contact! Control, we're on the Moon at Hadley Rille!"

We've landed about two kilometers from the canyon just to be safe. (We don't want to risk falling in.) Wasting no time, we are soon suited-up and standing outside on the surface of another world. Only twelve people in all of history have walked on the Moon, and the view above shows the strange kind of landscape that greeted them.

Quiet, desolate and dramatic. This surface has been un-disturbed by human footsteps for its entire four-and-one-half-billion-year history. After an awed and silent look around, we get down to business and climb into our moon buggy for the drive over to the canyon.

Could this really be a dried-up river valley? There is certainly no water down there now. Remember how on Earth a main canyon will have tributary streams branching into it? No sign of that here. We take some photos and gather up some rocks to take back. Weeks later analysis of the rocks on Earth will show that they have never been in contact with water. The Moon has been an airless desert for billions of years. The most likely explanation for this canyon is that it was carved out by a river — not of water, but of molten lava.

41 To the Moon

Working on the Moon

What is it like to work on the Moon?

Imagine yourself in ten layers of winter clothing with a fishbowl over your head, carrying a backpack with your oxygen supply, cooling system, and radio. You are totally cut off from the outside world. But you are also protected from it: from the Sun's blazing heat where it strikes the Moon, and the chilling cold where it doesn't; from an airless vacuum that would make your blood boil; from dust motes whizzing by at the speed of bullets.

You will need to wear this outfit for up to eight hours at a time as you explore the Moon's surface. This, of course, presents problems. Hungry? A compressed food bar is positioned inside your helmet for a quick nibble. Thirsty? Turn your head toward the strawlike tube mounted on the neck ring; a sip will bring up some refreshing orange drink. Need to use the bathroom? Luckily you have a urine collection device, as well as a giant diaper to prevent disasters.

You are also well equipped for your scientific duties. Various scoops, hammers, tongs, bags, and containers are attached to your space suit for collecting rocks. You also have a camera fitted to a bracket on your chest. Around your elbow is a wristwatch. And on your wrist is a small book that guides you through the planned activities while on the Moon.

Luckily, all this equipment —and you—weigh only one-sixth of your normal Earth weight. The reason is that the Moon is much smaller than Earth and exerts less gravity on objects. Moving around on the Moon is as easy and pleasant as bouncing across a trampoline.

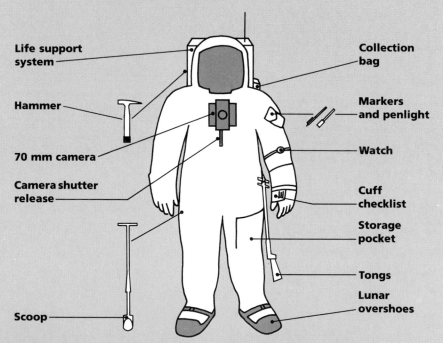

Life support system

Hammer

70 mm camera

Camera shutter release

Scoop

Collection bag

Markers and penlight

Watch

Cuff checklist

Storage pocket

Tongs

Lunar overshoes

Thus the Moon slowly reveals its secrets. During our three days on the surface we will drive for many kilometers collecting rocks and seeking out answers to some of the Moon's other secrets: How did it form—torn from the Earth?—captured as it passed in space?—condensed from the same cloud of dust that created the Earth? What caused the craters—volcanoes? —meteors? And our last question, as we look up into the cloudless black sky and glimpse our own blue home: Why is the Moon so utterly unlike the Earth?

We will be able to answer some of these questions a little later in the book. Meanwhile, the Apollo flight plan calls for us to climb back aboard the lunar module and take off for a rendezvous with the command module—from there to return to Earth. But for you and me this trip has just begun. We are about to set off instead to see more of our great and mysterious universe.

▼
High overhead and far away, the home of five billion humans is seen by two of their number on the Moon.

Chapter 4

Venus and Mercury

Before we continue our travels, let's make a few observations while we're still on the Moon.

If we stayed here long enough, nighttime would come and thousands of stars would spread out across the sky, just as they do on Earth. Since the Moon has no atmosphere the stars in the lunar sky shine with unusual brilliance. And we can see many thousands more than on even the darkest and clearest of Earth nights.

Something else is unusual about this night—it lasts for two weeks. This is because the Moon turns once on its axis in about twenty-eight Earth days, making the lunar days and nights last close to fourteen Earth days each.

If we managed to stay awake during the long lunar night, we would get to know the night sky quite well. If you've never paid much attention to the stars, then they all look pretty much alike. But close study soon brings out their differences. We can see bright stars, dim stars, yellow stars, blue stars, single stars, double stars and big clusters of stars.

But the most unusual stars of all are five very bright ones, and three much dimmer ones, that *move around*. They actually make slow loops and zigzags in the heavens, moving first one way and then the other. We might not notice this motion on our first lunar night, since these loops take several months. But given time, we would observe that these eight stars move about erratically and the other eight thousand, or eight million or however many you can count, don't.

The ancient Greeks were so struck by this that they gave these stars a special name, *planetes asteres*, which means "the wandering stars." You may not know ancient Greek but there is certainly a familiar word there: "planet." These unusual stars are the planets.

▲
Two brilliant planets lie in a line extending to the upper right of the Moon; they are Venus and Jupiter. Dimmer Saturn lies between them, almost directly above Venus. The other pinpoints of light are stars.

◄

(Opposite) ***These are much closer views of Venus—made from a spacecraft to show changes in the planet over a two-day period.***

The solar system. The planets get farther and farther apart the greater the distance we travel from the Sun. The outermost planet, Pluto, is shown at its greatest distance; but Pluto's elliptical orbit occasionally takes it slightly closer to the Sun than Neptune (see Chapter 8). Along the bottom is a line-up of the planets showing their relative sizes. All of the big planets are found in the outer solar system. Three of these gigantic worlds have ring systems.

▼

The ancients believed that the planets were gods. And the divine names that they assigned to them have come down to us today:

Mercury, the swiftest of the ancient gods, is also the fastest-moving planet.

Venus is the goddess of love, and the beautiful morning or evening star.

Mars, the god of war, is the planet that shines with a blood-red luster.

Jupiter, king of the gods, is the ruler of the night sky — the brilliant all-night planet.

And *Saturn*, Jupiter's father, is the slow-moving deposed king, surpassed in speed and splendor by his ambitious son.

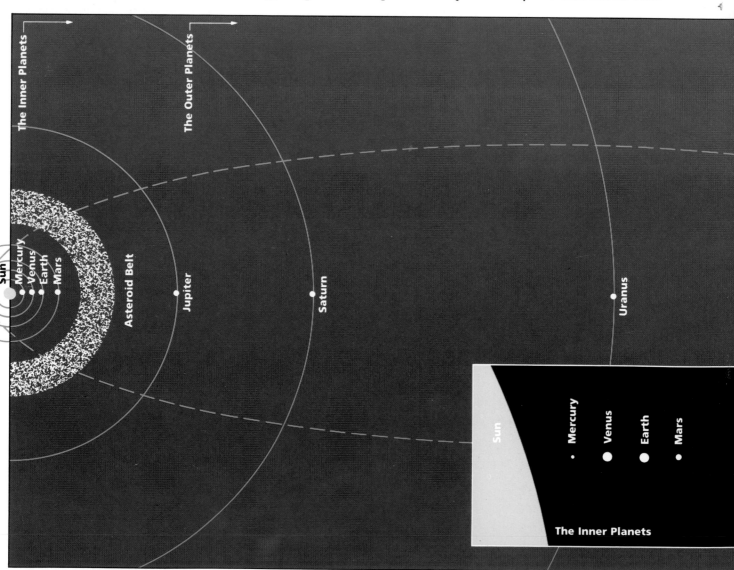

The three dim planets beyond Saturn — *Uranus, Neptune,* and *Pluto* — were discovered in more recent times with the aid of telescopes, but they were named after the old gods just the same.

What are the planets, really? We now know that unlike stars, which shine by their own light, the planets shine by reflected sunlight. They are other worlds that orbit the Sun, just as Earth does. And this is the secret of why they wander. In their great race around the Sun the planets move at different speeds. Venus passes Earth on an inside orbit while Mars falls behind in its slower outer orbit. Then swift Mercury races from behind to overtake them all. This continual shifting of the lead is the reason the planets appear to zig and zag in the sky.

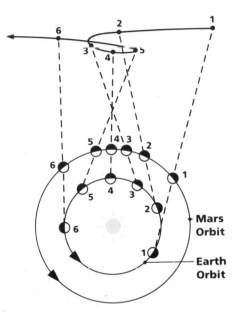

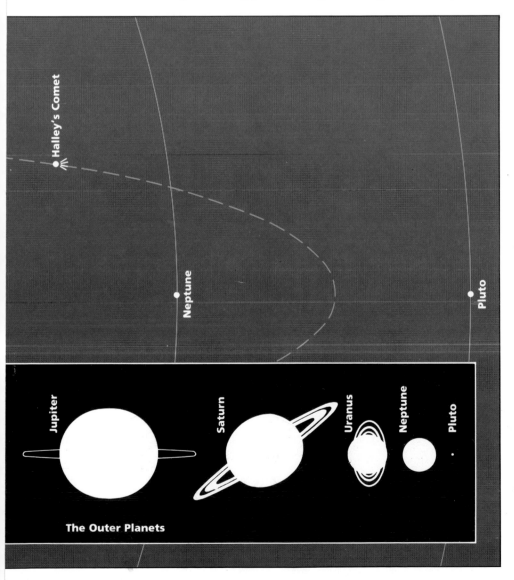

The Outer Planets

▲
A time exposure made in a planetarium previews the path Mars will follow in the constellation Sagittarius in 1986. Mars enters from the right in April, grows bright as the Earth gets closer, executes a loop, and exits at the left in October. The diagram demonstrates why we observe the loop. At first, Mars is moving ahead of Earth (points #1 and #2). But Earth is closer to the Sun and moves in a faster orbit; so it soon catches up. As Earth passes (#3 and #4), Mars seems to reverse direction. After a few weeks Mars again reverses direction (#5), closes the loop (#6), and heads out of the scene.

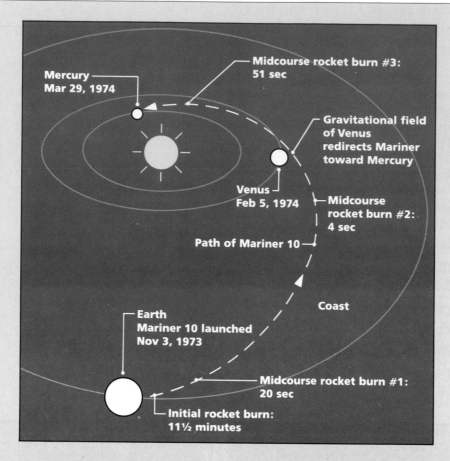

Mercury
Mar 29, 1974

Midcourse rocket burn #3:
51 sec

Gravitational field
of Venus
redirects Mariner
toward Mercury

Venus
Feb 5, 1974

Midcourse
rocket burn #2:
4 sec

Path of Mariner 10

Coast

Earth
Mariner 10 launched
Nov 3, 1973

Midcourse rocket burn #1:
20 sec

Initial rocket burn:
11½ minutes

Gravity Assist

How do you get two planets for the price of one? How does *Mariner 10* manage to combine Venus and Mercury in the same trip? It's not nearly as simple as stopping off in Washington on your way to New York.

On a trip to the planets a spaceship is given just enough of a boost to permit it to coast to its destination. Remember that there is no air resistance in space to slow a spaceship down, so for the greater part of its journey it burns no fuel at all. It took a total rocket burn of just over twelve minutes to send *Mariner 10* on a thirteen-week trip to Venus! Obviously, you have to aim very carefully during those few minutes.

As *Mariner 10* approaches Venus, the planet's gravity begins tugging at the spaceship, altering its course and changing its speed. Scientists have calculated that if Mariner arrives at a certain point 16,000 km (10,000 miles) from Venus at the correct time, then the spaceship's course will bend by exactly the right amount to reach Mercury fifty-two days later. Timing is important because planets are moving targets. Arrive a day early or a day late and your destination will be somewhere else.

(Above) Mariner 10's *fuel-saving path to Venus and Mercury.* (Left) *The* Mariner 10 *spacecraft. Note the sunshade to protect Mariner from the Sun's intense heat.*

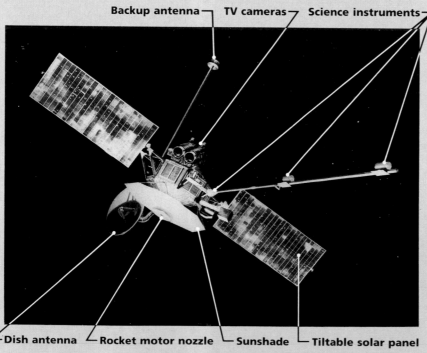

Backup antenna   TV cameras   Science instruments

Dish antenna   Rocket motor nozzle   Sunshade   Tiltable solar panel

If we were worried about finding another dead world like the Moon, then *Mariner*'s pictures give us hope—clouds!

The only trouble is that we can't see *through* the clouds. If this were Earth there would be plenty of clouds, it's true, but we could also see ocean and land. But these clouds are definite evidence of an atmosphere on Venus and that should be a good sign. Let's check some of our other measurements.

As *Mariner 10* passes behind Venus our radio signal to Earth cuts through the cloud layers, giving us a look at the structure of the atmosphere. The data is surprising: the cloud tops reach to 70 km (40 miles)—six times higher than Earth clouds. Slightly lower down, at 50 km, we find that the air pressure is the same as at Earth's surface, and it increases steadily as our radio signal cuts deeper.

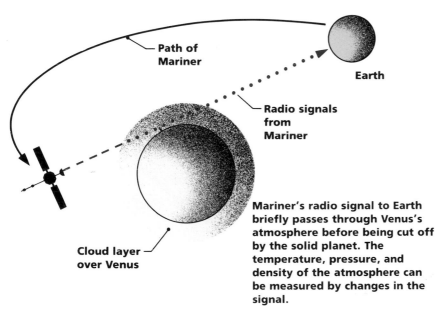

Path of Mariner

Earth

Radio signals from Mariner

Cloud layer over Venus

Mariner's radio signal to Earth briefly passes through Venus's atmosphere before being cut off by the solid planet. The temperature, pressure, and density of the atmosphere can be measured by changes in the signal.

Seconds later, *Mariner 10* swings behind the planet. Back at Control, scientists are able to measure the strength of our signal and determine that the air at the surface of Venus pushes down with one hundred times the force that it does on Earth. This is equivalent to the pressure at a depth of one kilometer in the ocean. We would be crushed if we tried to step onto such a world.

Venus, the so-called planet of love, gets even stranger. Analysis of other data shows that the surface temperature, day and night, hovers near 500 degrees Centigrade (900 degrees

Venus

- *Position:* **Second planet from the Sun**

- *Distance from Sun:* **108 million km (67 million miles)**

- *Length of year:* **7 months**

- *Length of day:* **4 months**

- *Diameter:* **12,000 km (7,500 miles— ⁹⁄₁₀ Earth's diameter)**

Note that a day on Venus lasts about one half of its year, which means that your birthday would fall every other day on the Venus calendar. Because Venus turns in the opposite direction from most other planets, the Sun rises in the west and sets in the east—if you could see it through the dense clouds.

Earth

Venus

Fahrenheit) — hot enough to melt lead! And those friendly-looking clouds are not water vapor but sulfuric acid, suspended in an atmosphere of almost pure carbon dioxide. No oxygen; hot enough to melt lead; certainly no living thing could survive on Venus. Perhaps no machine could either.

But machines have gone there. In 1982 *Venera 13,* the seventh Russian spaceship to land on Venus and the third to radio back photographs, operated in the hellish temperatures and pressures for over an hour and managed to take this picture.

▲

Venera 13 *reveals rocks and pebbles on Venus. In order to get as much scenery as possible in a single photograph, Venera's camera swiveled from the horizon in one direction, to the ground directly below, to the other horizon. Various parts of the spaceship are visible. The camera heat shield, ejected just after landing, is left of center; it is 20 cm (8 inches) wide.*

Then, like the other six landers, it went dead.

How are we to understand such a world in terms of our friendly Earth, or even by comparison with the cold and lifeless Moon? Other spaceships have gone to Venus to seek out answers. As we see above, *Venera 13* showed that the surface has rocks, pebbles, and dust. But what of mountains and other large-scale features? How do we detect them when we can't see through the clouds?

Actually, if we look with the right kind of light we *can* see through the clouds. Spaceships using radar, which is a form of light, have been able to peer through the atmosphere and

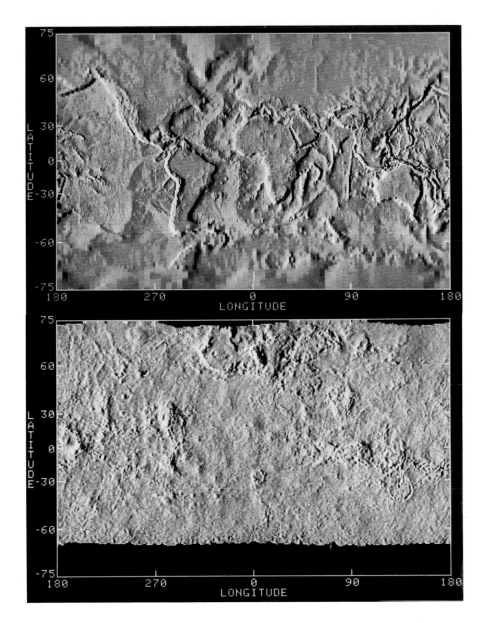

What does Venus look like under all the clouds? A radar spacecraft has orbited the planet and has made a rough map of the surface. Here we compare the Venus map (below) with a map of Earth's lithosphere showing the same level of detail (above). There don't seem to be any continents on Venus, but there are mountains, plains, and craters. Some of the mountains turn out to be volcanoes.

map the surface of Venus. These spaceships have discovered such familiar landforms as mountain chains, craters, and volcanoes. Needless to say, no oceans have been found on Venus. They would have turned to steam long ago.

From what we've learned looking at the Earth, it seems likely that the volcanoes on Venus produced the atmosphere. And so one piece of the puzzle falls into place. But many questions remain: Why is the air so hot and dense? Is the nearness of the Sun to blame? Will Mercury be even worse? The best way to find out is to press on.

Seven weeks and 30 million km (20 million miles) beyond

Mercury

- **Position:**
  First planet from the Sun

- **Distance from Sun:**
  58 million km
  (36 million miles)

- **Length of year:**
  3 months

- **Length of day:**
  2 months

- **Diameter:**
  4,900 km (3,000 miles —
  ⅖ Earth's diameter)

Being the closest planet to the Sun, Mercury has the smallest orbit, and therefore the shortest year — only three months long. When we reach the farthest planet in Chapter 8 we will find that a year out there lasts for *a thousand* Mercury years.

Earth   Mercury

▶

Mercury, the closest planet to the Sun.

Venus is Mercury, the closest planet to the Sun. Here, in the searing inner reaches of the solar system, the Sun looms nine times larger than in our Earth sky. Surely this sun-splashed planet is hotter than Venus.

As Mercury comes into range of our cameras, we see that it looks familiar. Haven't we seen this landscape before . . . ? A brief pass within 6,000 km (4,000 miles) shows that we are not mistaken.

This battered, pockmarked place looks just like the Moon! There are the old familiar craters — millions of them. And a look at Mercury's sharp, clean limb shows no sign of an atmosphere.

Mercury is like the Moon in more spectacular ways: it has a huge crater 1,300 km (800 miles) across, wider than the state of Texas! *Mariner 10* can just make out about half of this

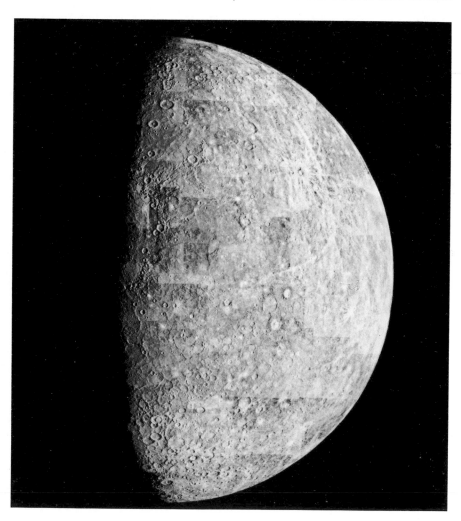

feature, but a similar crater on the Moon has been photographed in all of its detail.

Both features look like circular ripples in a pond after a stone has been dropped in. In fact, scientists believe that stones *did* create these craters. The "stones" were probably the size of Manhattan Island, weighing billions of tons and traveling through space at thousands of kilometers per hour. They were gigantic meteors.

Just as these big craters were gouged out by big meteors, it makes sense that the many small craters on Mercury and the Moon were created by small meteors. You have probably noticed that on a rocky beach there are thousands of small rocks for every boulder. Well, in space there are millions of small meteors for every Manhattan-sized one. Meteors of every size must have rained down onto Mercury and the Moon to create the variety of craters that we see. But why didn't this same "rain" fall on Earth?

We will get to this and other interesting questions in Chapter 6. But right now *Mariner 10* is taking Mercury's temperature.

Because Mercury is three times closer to the Sun than Earth, and twice as close as Venus, it seems a good bet that this well-baked planet is also the hottest. During our fly-by, Mariner's instruments are able to measure the late-afternoon temperature. The reading is a surprising 200 degrees C (400 degrees Fahrenheit)—hot enough to bake bread, perhaps, but not to melt lead. How could Mercury be cooler than Venus? Why is there no atmosphere? And why did so many meteors fall here and not on Earth?

Our first explorations beyond Earth have left us with more questions than answers. If we include our home planet, then we have looked at four worlds. Two are airless and cratered. Two are wrapped in a warming blanket of gases. Only one has liquid water at its surface.

Mariner 10 is trapped in a perpetual orbit near Mercury, so we must leave it behind to continue our investigations in another direction—away from the Sun, toward Mars and the outer planets.

What will those other "ancient gods" have in store . . . ?

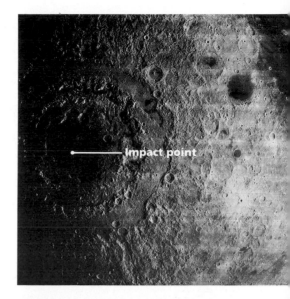

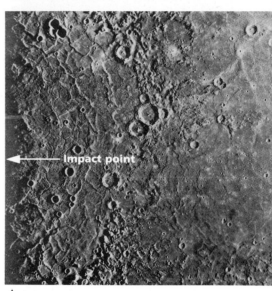

Texas-size craters on the Moon (top), and on Mercury (bottom). These enormous features are evidence of giant meteors flying through space. Note the ripples radiating from the meteor impact points.

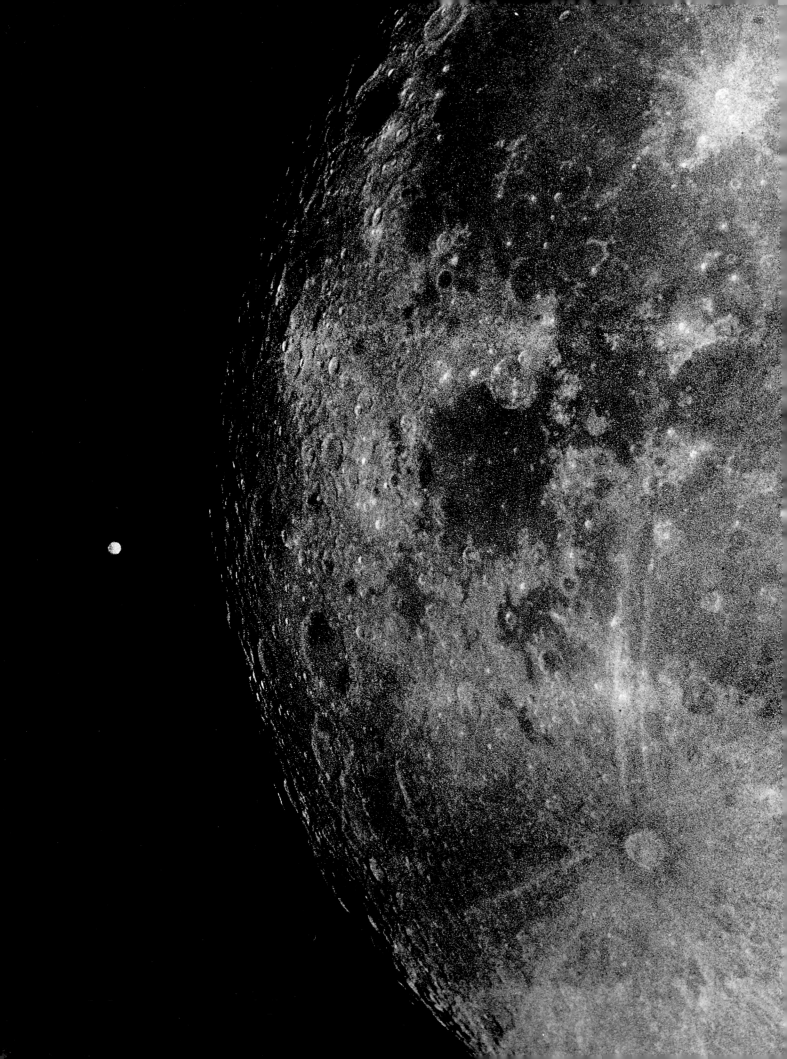

Chapter 5

Mars

Let's think back to the end of Chapter 2, when we were in Earth orbit on board the Shuttle. You may remember that we looked out the window and saw the Moon—380,000 km (240,000 miles) distant—as it rose over the Earth. It certainly seemed a very long way off then.

Now that we've been to Venus and Mercury, it's going to take a lot more to impress us.

Well, here it is. This view through a telescope (opposite page) shows a bright dot hovering over the Moon. Is it the Apollo lunar module getting ready to land? No. It is actually the mysterious Red Planet—Mars—rising 60 million km (40 million miles) beyond the Moon. Mars is the fourth planet as one moves outward from the Sun (after Mercury, Venus, and Earth). And Mars is our next stop as we continue our exploration of the solar system.

The planet Mars has captured the imaginations of countless writers of science fiction. In their stories there is no question that Mars is inhabited—and by an advanced civilization! Indeed, a hundred years ago some scientists were also convinced of this. They looked through the best telescopes of the day and thought they saw a complex network of canals, a sure sign of a technological society.

We now know that the "canals" were probably the result of eyestrain. But the question won't go away: Is Mars inhabited? Are there little green men there, or only little green microbes? Is there any kind of life there at all? The best way to answer this question is to go and have a look around.

A number of automatic spaceships have already gone to Mars, and we will stow away aboard one of them. To choose a spaceship we'll do what any sensible stowaway does—we'll look at the timetable.

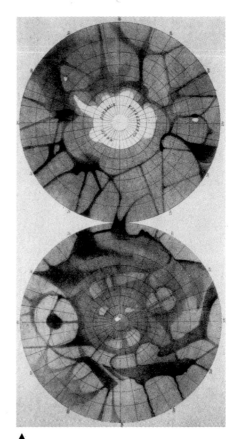

▲ **An 1879 map of Mars drawn by Italian astronomer, Schiaparelli. The network of connected lines were an optical illusion (not canals) and did not correspond to anything on the planet.**

◄ **(Opposite) A telescope on Earth shows Mars rising millions of kilometers beyond the Moon.**

Viking 1, *the first mission equipped to search for life on another planet, leaves for Mars.*

Timetable to Mars

Spacecraft	Arrival date	Mission
Mars 1 (USSR)	1963?	Contact lost halfway to Mars
Mariner 3 (USA)	——	Spacecraft died 8 hours after launch
Mariner 4 (USA)	1965	First successful Mars probe; took 21 close-up photos as it flew past
Zond 2 (USSR)	1965?	Contact lost
Mariner 6 and *7* (USA)	1969	Flew by; took another 101 pictures of Mars
Mariner 8 (USA)	——	Rocket malfunction sent this spacecraft into the Atlantic Ocean
Mariner 9 (USA)	1971	First spacecraft to orbit the Red Planet
Mars 2 and *3* (USSR)	1971	Orbited Mars and dropped probes to the surface; radio contact lost
Mars 4, 5, 6, and *7* (USSR)	1974	Orbiters (*Mars 4 & 5*) and surface probes (*Mars 6 & 7*); all except *Mars 5* failed
Viking 1 and *2* (USA)	1976	Two orbiters (51,539 photos) and first successful landers, which tested for life

There is no question that Mars is a popular destination, and our safest and best bet for passage looks like Viking. Two Viking spaceships arrived at Mars in 1976. Each had two parts: an orbiter and a lander. The orbiters took many thousands of photographs, and the landers were the first machines ever to touch down safely on the Martian surface. Indeed, according to our timetable, these landers were testing for life. This trip is beginning to look very promising.

So Viking it will be and off we go, riding a Titan-Centaur rocket into space for a ten-month voyage to the Red Planet . . .

We will have lots of free time, and this will give us a chance to make some predictions about what to expect on Mars. First of all, let's see if we can learn some lessons from the other worlds we have so far investigated.

Martians!

1898: Martians invade Earth for the first time in H. G. Wells's classic novel War of the Worlds.

1912: Peace reigns as Earthman John Carter marries Martian princess, Dejah Thoris, in "Under the Moons of Mars" by Edgar Rice Burroughs (creator of Tarzan of the Apes).

1930: Martians are causing trouble again, this time for comic-strip hero Buck Rogers.

Nonexistent Martians have been causing trouble for Earthlings since 1877. It was in that year that Italian astronomer Giovanni Schiaparelli observed the Red Planet through a telescope and saw a fine network of lines. He called these *canali,* Italian for channels, but this was mistranslated into English as "canals." If there were canals on Mars, then there must be Martians there to dig them. Professor Schiaparelli never meant this at all, but the idea caught on.

Many astronomers grew up reading science fiction stories about Mars, and they have wanted desperately to find life there. No one expected to find Dejah Thoris or the tiger-men that Buck Rogers battled, but scientists would be overjoyed just to find a simple plant or even a microbe. Such a discovery would mean that life got a start somewhere else besides Earth. And once life gets started, tiger-men, princesses, and canals could be just a few billion years of evolution away.

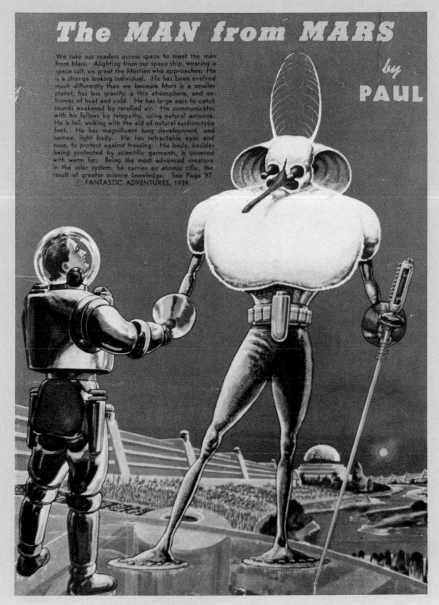

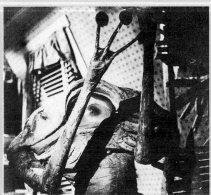

▲ *A visitor from Earth greets the man from Mars on the cover of* Fantastic Adventures *magazine, 1939.*

◄ *A Martian examines an Earth dwelling in the movie version of* War of the Worlds.

**Earth's mass =
6,000,000,000,000,000,000,000,000 kg
(about 7,000
million million million tons)**

**Mercury's mass =
¹⁄₁₈ (5.5%) of
Earth's mass**

**Venus's mass =
⁴⁄₅ (80%) of
Earth's mass**

**Moon's mass =
¹⁄₈₀ (1.2%) of
Earth's mass**

This is how Earth, Mercury, Venus, and the Moon would look if we lined them up, side by side. Two have atmospheres. Two don't. Mercury and the Moon are smaller, and look roughly the same size. Likewise, Venus and Earth are bigger, and are also similar in size. What can we learn from this? One thing is that the bigger planets are the ones with atmospheres. But why should this be?

Well, let's look at the number below each planet. This is the planet's weight, or what scientists call its "mass." Here it is given as a fraction of Earth's mass, which is *six million million million million* kilograms. It is often true that big things are heavier than small things, and it's true here. Earth is about twenty times heavier than Mercury. Venus is seventy times heavier than the Moon. The worlds without atmospheres are clearly the lightweights.

Now why should a big, heavy planet have an atmosphere while a small planet does not? Perhaps only planets of a certain size have volcanoes—which spew out their gases to create atmospheres. This is a good guess, but think about the case of the Moon. Hadley Rille, the lunar canyon that we visited in Chapter 3, was created by a river of molten lava. Presumably, this lava came from a volcano of some sort, so we know that at one time the Moon had volcanic gases. But we also know that the Moon has no atmosphere. If the Moon had the necessary gases but they never formed into an atmosphere, then what happened to them?

The answer lies in the close connection between mass (weight) and gravity. Less mass means less gravity. A small world has less gravity than a large one. If you've seen films of astronauts on the Moon, then you've seen them bouncing around on a world with gravity one-sixth as strong as Earth's.

Lunar gravity pulls down not only on astronauts, but on *everything*—including gases—with less force. And the gases, being already very light, just drift away into space. A small world like the Moon probably had the makings of an atmosphere at one time, but the gases escaped. There was not enough gravity to hold them down. Because Mercury is more massive than the Moon, it has more gravity, but still not enough to hold on to a respectable atmosphere—especially under the hot conditions on Mercury's surface.

Here we have a very important law about the planets: Atmospheres depend on mass. We cannot hope to find an atmosphere on a lightweight world like the Moon.

Now let's put Mars into the lineup with Earth, Venus, and the rest, and see if we can guess whether it will have an atmosphere or not.

▲ *Astronaut John Young makes a leaping salute to the flag in the Moon's weak gravity field.*

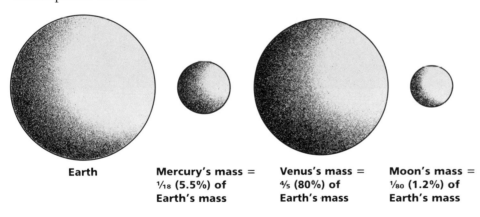

| Earth | Mercury's mass = 1/18 (5.5%) of Earth's mass | Venus's mass = 4/5 (80%) of Earth's mass | Moon's mass = 1/80 (1.2%) of Earth's mass | Mars's mass = 1/9 (11%) of Earth's mass |

Mars looks like a kind of halfway planet. It is halfway in size between the Moon and Earth. Its mass is nine times greater than the Moon's, but only one-ninth of Earth's. Using a little arithmetic, scientists are able to calculate that any gases emitted from the interior of Mars should have collected into a modest atmosphere.

This is good news, but what of other signs favorable for life? After all, an atmosphere is not enough. Think of the boiling pea-soup atmosphere we encountered on Venus. So far the only planet where we've found life is Earth. Earth is also the only planet where we've found water at the surface. Could there also be water on Mars?

Mars

- **Position:**
  Fourth planet from the Sun

- **Distance from Sun:**
  230 million km
  (140 million miles)

- **Length of year:**
  Almost two Earth years

- **Length of day:**
  24 hours 37 minutes

- **Diameter:**
  6,800 km (4,200 miles —
  ½ Earth's diameter)

Notice that the length of a Mars day is remarkably close to an Earth day. Mars is also tilted on its axis, like Earth, and therefore has seasons. These coincidences caused some people to jump to conclusions, assuming that Mars resembled Earth in more complicated ways, and therefore had rivers, lakes, plants, animals . . . and Martians.

Earth   Mars

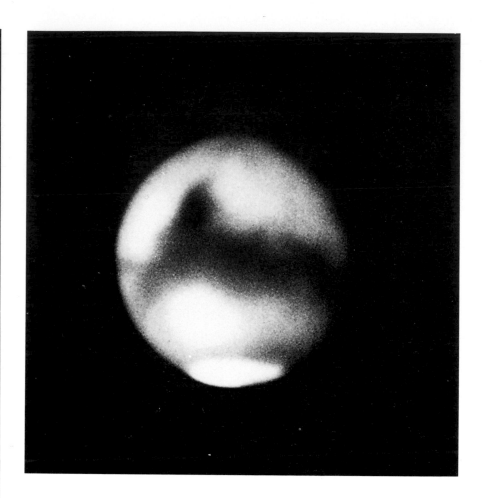

(Top) *Mars seen from spaceship* **Earth,** *and* **(opposite page)** *Mars seen from spaceship* **Viking.**

This is Mars viewed through a telescope on Earth. We can see a pretty clear sign of something that might be water. Can you spot it? Ice! There is an icy-looking white patch around the south pole, much like the polar caps on Earth.

So even before we've arrived at Mars, we have good reason to expect an atmosphere and possibly water. These are the basic conditions for life. And this is why scientists have kept up such a steady schedule of flights to the Red Planet. Will we find life when we get there? We are about to find out. Ten months' traveling may seem like a long time, but it passes quickly in the eternity of space.

At one-half million km (300,000 miles) the opposite page shows our view from Viking. Compare it with the view we just saw through a telescope on Earth.

Everything is coming into much sharper focus. That certainly looks like winter frost in the south. And could those be clouds trailing from the dark spot in the north?

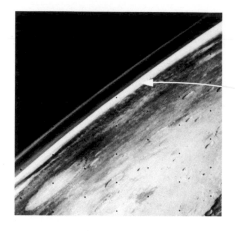

▲
A Viking spacecraft orbiting Mars checks the limb for signs of an atmosphere (top) and looks down on a cratered region (bottom).

▶

Viking spots a group of canyons. This photo shows the usual information that accompanies a space image. Along the top is the unique picture number. At the bottom are tables of geographic data and computer processing graphs.

Viking will enter orbit with the same maneuver that we used back at the Moon. Our speed as we approach is 14,000 km/hour (9,000 miles/hour). We must slow down to 10,000 km/hour in order to be captured by the Martian gravity. This is one-third less than orbital velocity back at Earth, and is another demonstration that Mars is less massive: less speed is required to orbit it. We apply the brakes in the usual way by firing our rocket against our direction of travel. Thirty-eight minutes later we are making long, slow loops around the Red Planet.

Looking down from orbit, we see that Mars really is a kind of halfway world. *Some* features look like Earth, and *some* like the other planets. Here is the Martian limb showing a hazy layer of clouds, much like Earth's.

And here is a battered region of craters that could easily be Mercury.

Here are canyons similar to Hadley Rille on the Moon.

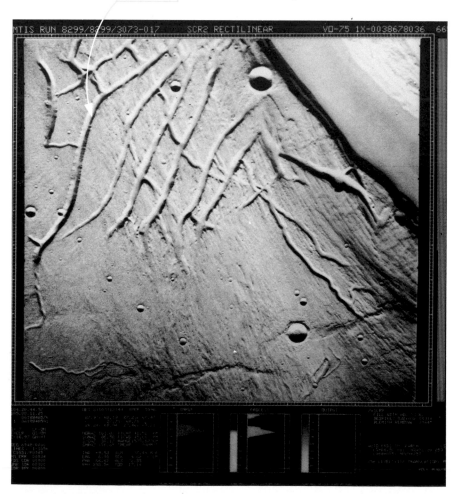

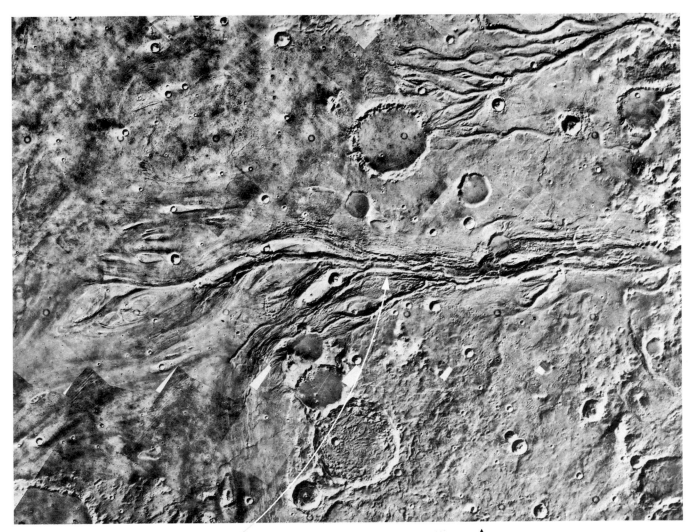

And *here* are features that, until now, we have only seen on Earth — river systems!

These are no lava canyons. Look at the way tributary streams branch into the main channel. This is the telltale pattern of flowing water. Could we have found evidence of a hydrosphere on another world?

The more we look over Mars, the more of these stream systems we find. Yet something is funny, because there doesn't seem to be water in them. Nor do there seem to be any lakes or oceans where these streams are emptying.

Around and around we go, looking for the answer to this riddle. And in the search — as so often happens in exploration — we stumble on an even bigger riddle. Mars has a canyon that is so big it could not possibly have been created by water.

▲
Two branching river systems flow across the Martian surface without a drop of water. The picture is 300 km (200 miles) across — the distance between New York and Washington, D.C.

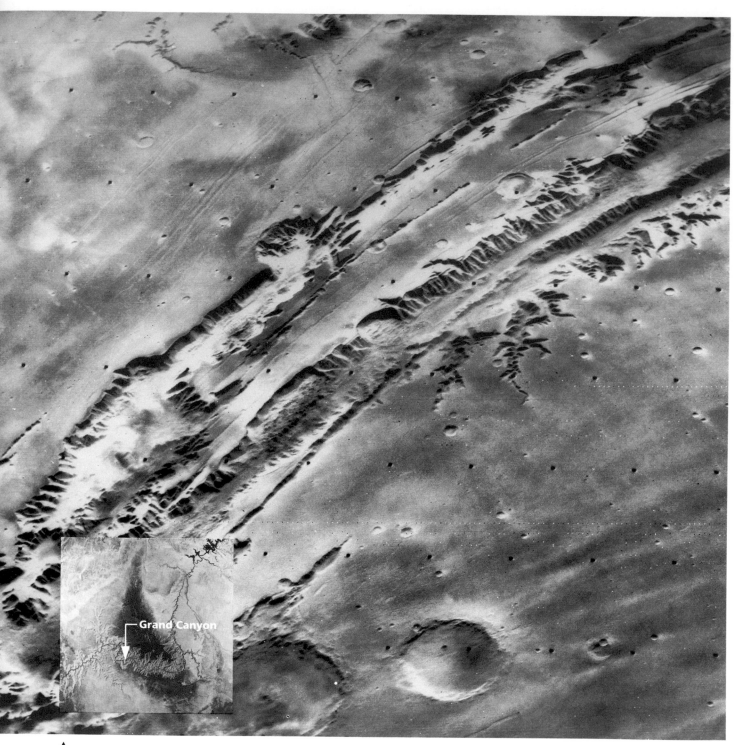

Grand Canyon

▲

Mariner Valley on Mars would reach across the continental United States. Here we see one-quarter of it, compared with the Grand Canyon at the same scale.

Stretching across the page is the solar system's largest canyon. Earth's Grand Canyon, which we saw back in Chapter 2, is shown at the lower left as it would look if we could set it down next door. No longer does it look so grand.

And as if this weren't enough, several orbits later we find that Mars has the solar system's largest volcano!

Earth's biggest volcano, Mauna Loa on the island of Hawaii, is shown as *it* would appear next to this Mars giant.

▲
Earth's largest volcano would almost fit inside the crater atop Mount Olympus on Mars. Both are shown at the same scale as the two canyons opposite.

Astronauts on Mars

After America's success at sending astronauts to the Moon in 1969, the space agency—NASA—began looking into the possibility of sending astronauts to Mars. This is like deciding, after a one-week camping trip, that you're going to try a *two-year* trip next.

In your mind think about what you would take on a two-year camping trip on Earth. Now consider what you would need for a two-year trip in space, for this is how long it takes to go to Mars and return. In space there is no air to breathe, no water to drink, no firewood; there are no streams to fish or berries to pick; everything you need to stay alive must be brought along in a two-year supply.

Mission planners had to consider the rocket power needed to send all of these supplies and a crew to Mars. To accomplish this job a single rocket would have to be six times larger than the *Saturn 5* (see page 6), the largest rocket ever launched.

There are other problems. How would the astronauts be rescued if their equipment failed? How would two years of weightlessness affect their bodies? What would the crew do to fill the long hours during the trip out and back?

But these problems are no more serious than those faced by explorers in the age of sailing ships.

No nation has yet announced plans to send astronauts to Mars. The trip will be very expensive, but it *can* be done. It is the next big adventure for explorers with an urge to step out onto a new world and explore it themselves.

◄

Artist Paul Hudson has imagined the scene as astronauts first step out onto the Red Planet. Here the pioneer space explorers are unloading cargo from their Mars lander.

Ice, clouds, craters, rilles, dry riverbeds, giant canyons and volcanoes. How are we to make sense of all this? The solar system seems to be getting ever stranger as we plow deeper and deeper into it. We have evidence that at least Mars has *frozen* water—its ice caps. And it seems to have had liquid water at one time. Unfortunately, Viking's instruments tell us that Mars is now too cold and the atmosphere too thin to allow liquid water at the surface. Indeed, much of the ice at the Martian south pole is *dry* ice—frozen carbon dioxide—at a temperature far below the freezing point of water. What could these harsh conditions mean for the possibility of life?

Our Viking lander is ready to take the plunge and find out. We have carefully selected a landing site near the mouth of the dried-up river system shown below.

This area once had all the advantages of a rich river delta—one of the most fertile locations for life on our own Earth. We shouldn't expect green fields and forests on Mars (and certainly not little green men!), for we know that the water they would need to survive is long gone. But Viking is ready to look for more subtle signs of life—tiny microbes and spores.

▼
The Viking Lander testing its shovel on Earth. The shovel retracts like a tape measure to deposit soil in an onboard analyzer.

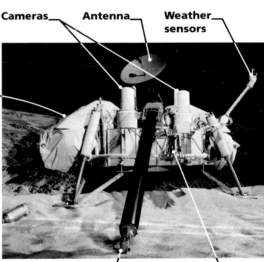

Cameras — Antenna — Weather sensors

Automatic shovel ⌐ Descent rocket ⌐ (1 of 3)

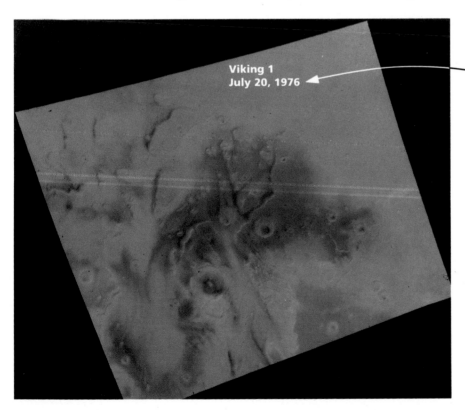

Viking 1
July 20, 1976 ◄

◄
Target for Viking 1. A Martian river flowing from the bottom of the picture once poured billions of tons of sediment into the region where Viking will set down. Was there ever life there? Is there life there still . . .?

The surface of the Red Planet. As on the Moon and Venus, we see plenty of rocks, but no trace of life. In the foreground are trenches dug by Viking to obtain soil for analysis aboard the spacecraft.

These could be the beginnings, or perhaps the end, of a great chain of life such as we ourselves are part of. And Viking has a sophisticated on-board laboratory to test for these very links in the chain.

So down we go . . .

It's a familiar Earthlike scene. We could almost be in the desert southwest of the United States. How does this landscape compare with the surfaces of the Moon and Venus? Without doubt Mars is far more inviting. Now, turn on your personal life detectors. What do your eyes tell you? Not a shrub, cactus, or blade of grass.

Viking's automatic shovel extends, and scoops up a tiny sample of the Red Planet. The on-board laboratory will test it

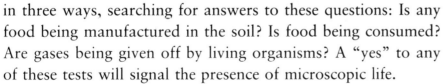
600 700 800 900 1000

▲
Martian soil sits in the funnels leading down into Viking's automatic laboratory.

in three ways, searching for answers to these questions: Is any food being manufactured in the soil? Is food being consumed? Are gases being given off by living organisms? A "yes" to any of these tests will signal the presence of microscopic life.

At first the results are encouraging, and scientists are ready to announce that they've discovered life on Mars. But it's a false alarm; it's only the Martian minerals that are lively. The tests produce a burst of oxygen, which then dies down. Scientists recognize that this is just a chemical reaction, like when lemon juice is added to baking soda. (Try it sometime—the mixture bubbles vigorously for a few seconds.)

There is no life in the red dirt—at least, no life as we know it. . . .

Chapter 6

Understanding the Inner Planets

In the past three chapters we have visited a group of worlds known as the inner planets. These are the four planets, and one moon, closest to the Sun. Our constant guide on this voyage has been our knowledge of Earth. At each new world we have asked, How does this place compare with our home planet? At every stop we have been fascinated . . . but disappointed. Truly, there's no place like home.

One way to summarize our findings is to make a chart.

	Lithosphere	Atmosphere	Hydrosphere	Biosphere
Mercury	yes			
Venus	yes	yes		
Earth	yes	yes	yes	yes
Moon	yes			
Mars	yes	yes	maybe	

The chart shows only too well what we now know through hard months of space travel. Earth alone has the unique conditions that make life as we know it possible. Mars comes close, but frozen water and thin air are not enough. Everything has to be just right—temperature, pressure, oxygen, water. We might wonder why everything worked out just right on Earth.

Another way of asking this question is, What went wrong with the other worlds? Why are the Moon and Mercury covered with craters? What happened to the water that once ran over Mars? Why is the atmosphere on Venus so thick? These are questions we have asked in the course of our travels, and before we journey even deeper into the solar system, we should try to answer them.

◄

(Opposite) The rocky worlds of the inner solar system. Along the top are Mercury and the Moon. At the bottom—Venus and Mars. The blue Earth is in the center.

A meteor burns up in Earth's atmosphere.

Think back to Chapter 3 when we gazed down at the cratered face of the Moon—or to Chapter 4 when we were surprised by the same battered landscape on Mercury. Why are some worlds covered with craters and others not?

The Moon and Mercury are by far the most heavily cratered worlds we've seen. Neither has an atmosphere. Could there be a connection?

It may help to think for a minute of the Apollo command module. If you recall, it comes equipped with a heat shield so it can enter Earth's atmosphere without burning up. But what is the situation for a meteor flying through space? It has no heat shield. When it encounters a planetary atmosphere, it will be destroyed in a flash of flame. On Earth these flaming meteors can be seen as "shooting stars."

But when flying toward Mercury or the Moon, a meteor doesn't have this problem—there's no atmosphere to penetrate. The meteor will plunge straight to the ground and make a crater.

This certainly looks like the answer to our question. You might wonder, though, about Meteor Crater in Arizona, or the craters on Mars and Venus. How did *they* get there?

Imagine for a minute that Earth, Mars, and Venus are as heavily battered as the Moon. This is no joke—they once were. Scientists believe that billions of years ago an incredible number of meteors were hurtling through space, raining down on every planet and moon. An atmosphere was little protection in those days because the meteors were so big that they plowed right through to the ground before the atmosphere could destroy them.

And so *all* of the inner planets were once covered with craters. The difference is that on those planets with atmospheres, erosion went to work wearing them away. On Earth, the craters were almost completely erased by the forces of wind, rain, oceans, rivers, and ice (and also by earthquakes and volcanoes). These processes worked less thoroughly on Venus and Mars, so a large number of craters still remain there.

Fortunately, the ancient rain of giant meteors has died down, but an occasional big one will still fall, making it all the way to the ground. Meteor Crater on Earth was formed 25,000 years ago in this way.

Meteorites

On November 8, 1982, at 9:17 in the evening, Robert and Wanda Donahue of Wethersfield, Connecticut were sitting quietly at home watching M*A*S*H on television. Suddenly there was a muffled explosion — "like a truck coming through the front door." Their house had been struck by a meteorite from space!

Luckily, no one was hurt, and the house was only slightly damaged. Amazingly, a house less than two miles from the Donahues' had been struck by a meteorite eleven years earlier.

Meteorites are meteors that reach the Earth's surface without completely burning up. They range in size from tiny dust specks to huge boulders. Most of them probably originate in the asteroid belt, where collisions between asteroids produce many small particles.

Scientists estimate that every day about 1 million kg (200 tons) of meteorites fall to the Earth. Most fall in the oceans, but some strike near populated areas, and only a *very, very* few are big enough to endanger any people.

So don't worry. In all of recorded history only one person has been injured by a meteorite — Mrs. E. Hulitt Hodges, while napping on her sofa in Sylacauga, Alabama, in 1954; her leg was bruised.

▲

A fireman looks at the hole made by a grapefruit-sized meteorite in the living room ceiling of Robert and Wanda Donahue. The meteorite bounced in the direction of the camera, into the dining room.

So it is that planets with atmospheres manage to protect themselves from small meteors *and* erode the craters left by really big ones. We should remember that when we look at a heavily cratered world we are really looking back in time, at an ancient surface that has experienced almost no erosion for billions of years.

The tangled, dark gray lines (top photo) are dry channels in eastern Washington State. Thousands of years ago a glacial ice dam burst, sending floodwaters pouring across the scene. A complicated system of valleys was created in a matter of days. A similar flood could be behind the channels on Mars (bottom photo). Both pictures are 150 km (90 miles) across.

Thinking back to some of the puzzles in the last chapter, we might wonder what happened to the water that once ran over the surface of Mars. Measurements from Viking tell us that Mars is too cold and has insufficient air pressure to keep water in a liquid state. How could water ever have flowed? We know that it must have done so, in order to create the many Martian stream systems.

Scientists have come up with a surprising explanation: meteors. According to this theory, some of the giant meteors that struck Mars exploded with enough heat to melt underground ice. Water rushed across the surface with great force before evaporating. In this way a complicated system of channels and valleys was created.

Such catastrophic flooding happened at least once on Earth, when a natural ice dam broke during a prehistoric glacial period, releasing the waters of a huge lake. The scoured landscape is still visible in eastern Washington State.

Evidence for Earth's ancient flood gave scientists the idea that a similar catastrophe might explain the Mars channels.

The giant canyon and volcano on Mars could not have been created so quickly. Scientists believe that these features, and others like them, formed gradually over hundreds of millions of years. They were probably created as stresses in the Martian lithosphere tore open the surface in one location (making the canyon), and allowed lava to seep to the surface in other areas (making volcanoes). Perhaps the stresses were caused by changes in the lithosphere due to heating and cooling in the interior of the planet, but no one is sure.

Our last question about the inner planets takes us back to Venus to try to understand why its atmosphere is so thick and inhospitable. Believe it or not, the answer also explains why life is possible on Earth.

Billions of years ago Earth's atmosphere was nearly pure carbon dioxide — as the atmosphere on Venus is now. Earth came very close to turning into another Venus, *except* Earth was just cool enough so that water vapor in the air was able to condense. This created the oceans. Since carbon dioxide is soluble in water, enormous amounts of this gas dissolved into the sea.

But perhaps Venus was never cool enough to form oceans. Instead, the carbon dioxide gas stayed in the air. An important property of this gas is that it traps heat that would otherwise escape into space. This forced temperatures on Venus higher and higher. Because glass in greenhouses acts in the same way to trap heat, this phenomenon is called the "greenhouse effect." On Venus it's so bad that it's called the *runaway* greenhouse effect.

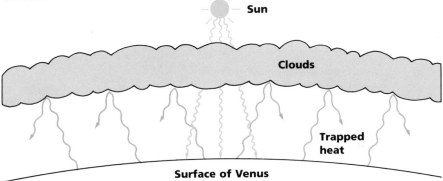

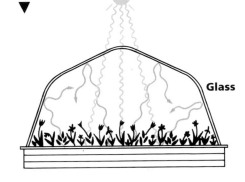

The greenhouse effect. In a greenhouse, short-wavelength radiation from the Sun enters through the transparent glass and warms the inside, turning to long-wave heat radiation that cannot escape. The same principle is at work on Venus (left). The clouds allow sunlight through, but prevent heat from escaping. ▼

Incidentally, this runaway heating explains why Venus is hotter than Mercury. Mercury has no atmosphere to trap and hold the Sun's energy, and is thus able to reflect much of its heat back into space. And so Mercury is cooler than Venus, even though it is twice as close to the Sun.

Runaway heating never happened on Earth because most of the carbon dioxide was dissolved in the sea. And it was there, in warm sunlit waters, that early life forms developed. Primitive organisms absorbed carbon dioxide from the water and released oxygen. Slowly, this new gas mixed with the air. Millions of years went by and the atmosphere became the vital mixture that gives life to all oxygen-breathing creatures—including us.

Little by little, we are beginning to make sense out of our solar system. We have seen how a planet's mass determines if it will have an atmosphere. We have seen how meteors batter the surfaces of worlds without atmospheres, and how they might have caused sudden floods on Mars. We have seen how liquid water can change poisonous air into the breath of life.

But we haven't seen everything. After all, we still have five planets to go. And out there, beyond Mars, giant worlds are waiting, holding the last few pieces of the puzzle.

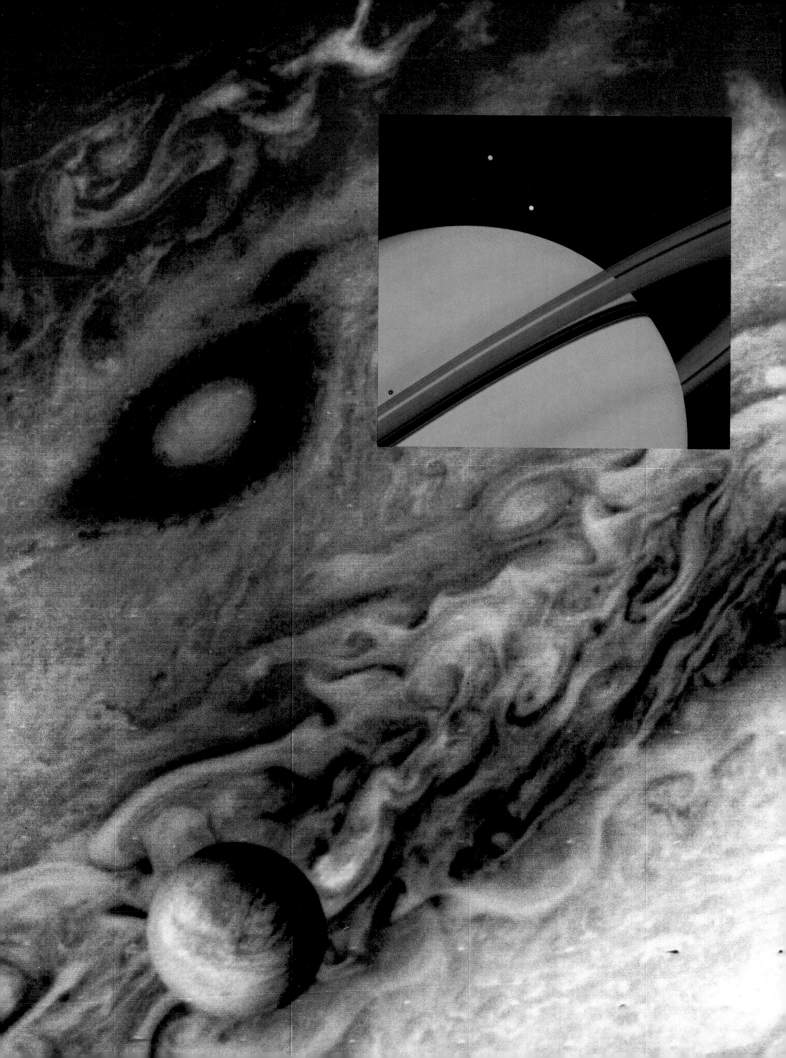

Chapter 7

The Giant Planets

In 1977 two Voyager spaceships were launched from Earth on a journey to the distant outer planets and beyond, a journey that still continues. In this chapter we will accompany the Voyagers as they fly within 350,000 km (220,000 miles) of Jupiter in 1979, and as they pass by the ringed planet, Saturn, almost two years later.

Then we will say good-bye to *Voyager 1* as it follows a northerly route past Saturn, taking it out of the realm of the planets. But the adventures of *Voyager 2* continue within the solar system, as it flies by Uranus in 1986, and Neptune in 1989. Since 1986 has not yet arrived, we will look at information about Uranus obtained from observations with Earth telescopes. You will have a chance to test your space explorer's skills by making your own predictions about what Voyager will find. Then in 1989 you can do the same for Neptune as Voyager passes the last of the giant planets—some 4 billion km (and 12 years) from Earth.

(Opposite) *Close-up of a moon orbiting high over Jupiter's clouds.* **(Inset)** *Saturn and two of its moons.*

◄

▼

The route of the Voyagers, mapped in an overhead view of the solar system. Note how Jupiter's gravity bends the trajectories in the direction of Saturn—and how Saturn sends Voyager 2 on to Uranus and Neptune.

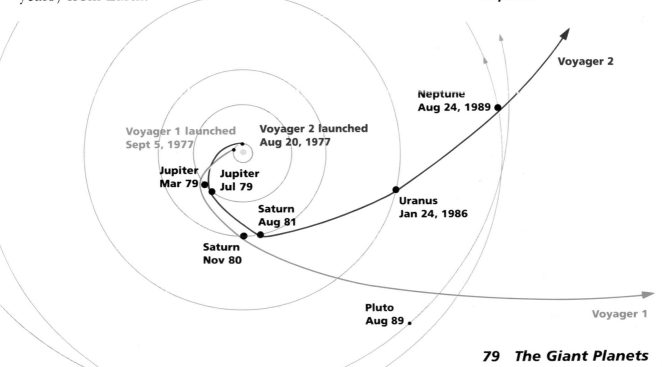

Voyager 2

Neptune
Aug 24, 1989 ●

Voyager 1 launched
Sept 5, 1977

Voyager 2 launched
Aug 20, 1977

Jupiter
Mar 79 ●

Jupiter
Jul 79

Uranus
Jan 24, 1986

Saturn
Aug 81

Saturn
Nov 80

Pluto
Aug 89 .

Voyager 1

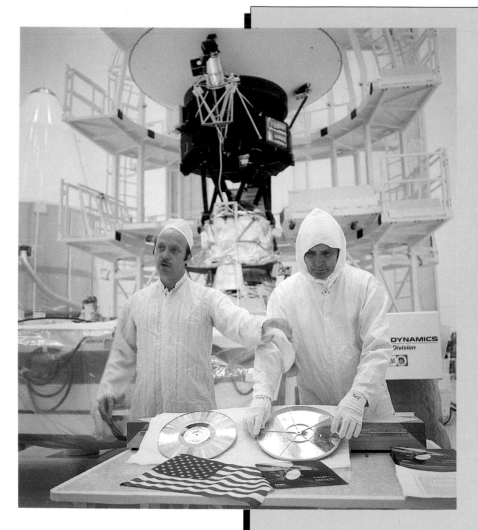

Gold Record

Long after their nuclear batteries die and they cease communicating with Earth, the two Voyager spacecraft will sail on. There is almost nothing to stop them. But suppose something does stop them—a faraway star surrounded by a planetary system, or a spaceship coming from another direction. Suppose intelligent beings find one of these contraptions from Earth. How will they know it's from Earth? How will they know what Earth *is*? The answers are on a gold-plated record, similar to a videodisc, that each Voyager carries attached to its side. If Voyager's alien captors can figure out how to play the record, they will be entertained for two hours with a rich selection of sounds, pictures, and messages from our home planet.

And they may just want to come for a visit.

▲

Technicians prepare the gold-plated "Sounds of Earth" record and a U.S. flag for storage on Voyager 2 (seen in the background). An identical record was placed on Voyager 1.

And what of the very last of the known planets—Pluto? Unfortunately, no spaceships are aimed for this distant outpost, so we must rely on what little information we can get from telescopes. In the next chapter we will focus on this tiny world, and in the process, discover that our explorations have barely begun.

But we're getting ahead of our story.

Our story begins in the late summer of 1977. Jimmy Carter is in the White House. The Yankees and the Red Sox are battling it out for first place in the American League East. Luke Skywalker and Darth Vader are battling it out in a new movie called *Star Wars*. And in Florida, two spaceships are taking off on an adventure to the end of the solar system . . .

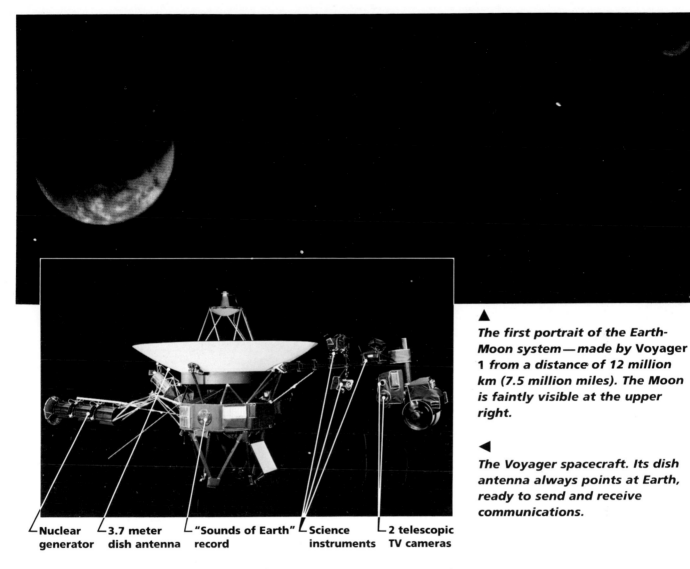

Nuclear generator   **3.7 meter dish antenna**   **"Sounds of Earth" record**   **Science instruments**   **2 telescopic TV cameras**

▲
The first portrait of the Earth-Moon system — made by Voyager 1 from a distance of 12 million km (7.5 million miles). The Moon is faintly visible at the upper right.

◄

The Voyager spacecraft. Its dish antenna always points at Earth, ready to send and receive communications.

Two weeks after leaving Earth, *Voyager 1* turns around and snaps a remarkable picture. It shows the Earth and the Moon together in a single frame. Back in Chapter 3 we crossed between these two worlds and thought we were really going places. But in order to get to Jupiter, Voyager must travel 3,000 times the Earth-Moon distance. Saturn is *6,000* times this distance; Uranus, *13,000*; Neptune, *20,000*! A football field is 20,000 times the length of this line (—), which should give you an idea of how much farther Neptune is than the Moon.

After just three months, the two Voyagers cross the orbit of Mars. Jupiter is next. But first we must pass through the asteroid belt—430 million km (270 million miles) of drifting, rocky debris.

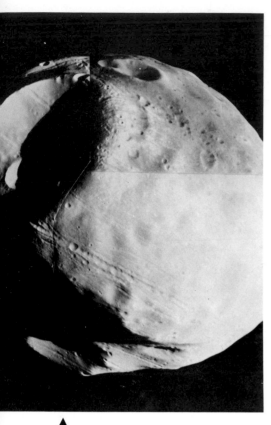

▲

Asteroids probably look very much like this oddly shaped moon of Mars, photographed by Viking. In fact, it is likely that this moon was an asteroid that was captured into orbit around Mars. Its diameter is 20 km (12 miles), making it an asteroid of medium size.

Many scientists believe that the asteroid belt is a kind of abandoned planetary construction site. All of the pieces are there, but they were never put together. Asteroids are the pieces—they are giant chunks of rock, sometimes hundreds of kilometers in diameter. Because each asteroid exerts a small gravitational tug on its fellow asteroids, all of them should have collected into a single planet over the course of millions of years. In fact, other planets may have formed in this way. But for some reason these rocks between Mars and Jupiter never got it together. No one is quite sure why.

Happily, the Voyagers sail through unscathed. The asteroid belt is probably no more dangerous than the Atlantic Ocean, where there is the hazard of an occasional iceberg.

The people of the ancient world could not have known it, but the planet that they named for the king of the gods *is* the king. Jupiter is the largest planet in the solar system. How large? On the opposite page we see how it looks next to Earth.

It's enormous. If Jupiter were hollow, 1,300 Earths would fit inside. And if Jupiter were made of the same stuff as Earth, it would be 1,300 times heavier. But look at the mass: the giant planet is just over *300* times the mass of Earth. Our only conclusion can be that it's made of some very lightweight material. As early as the 1930s scientists reasoned that Jupiter is made almost entirely of hydrogen and helium, the lightest of all elements. They were proved correct when the first spaceship flew past the planet in 1973.

This is something new. Until now, all of the worlds we've seen have been made of rock. Think of the surfaces of the Moon,

Venus, and Mars. Rocks. Even the asteroids are rocky. We will soon see that this is not the case in the outer solar system. We are about to enter a realm of gaseous giants. But before we get to the first—and biggest—of these, let's think about why this is happening.

One very important clue is the Sun. You may not have noticed, but it seems to be getting smaller and smaller. When Voyager passed the orbit of Mars, the Sun appeared only half as large as it does from Earth. Soon we will reach Jupiter and the Sun will look only one twenty-fifth as big. At Saturn: one hundredth. At Uranus: one four-hundredth.

And so on . . . the Sun grows ever smaller and colder, its gravity reaching out with less and less force.

Now, if the Sun had anything to do with the formation of the planets, we would expect the really big planets to form farther away, where the Sun's powerful gravity was less competition. And if the Sun's heat were any influence, then very light gases would tend to collect at great distances from the Sun. This is because solar radiation, which exerts a weak but steady pressure, would over time push hydrogen and helium into the outer solar system. So it makes sense to find big, gaseous planets out there.

A little later we will look more closely into the origins of the planets. But right now Voyager is showing us a little added attraction at Jupiter.

Jupiter

- **Position:**
  Fifth planet from the Sun

- **Distance from Sun:**
  **780 million km
  (480 million miles)**

- **Length of year:**
  12 Earth years

- **Length of day:**
  9 hours 50 minutes

- **Diameter:**
  **143,000 km (89,000 miles
  —11 times Earth's
  diameter)**

Oddly enough, the largest planet in the solar system spins the fastest and therefore has the shortest day—about ten hours. 10,565 of these brief days fit into the long Jupiter year.

Jupiter's mass =
318 times Earth's mass

Jupiter   Earth

One month away from our closest pass, Jupiter looks beautiful. Look more closely: there are two small "worlds" around the giant planet. There's a red one in front and a white one off to the right. These two worlds, plus two others that we can't see in this picture, were discovered in 1610 by the Italian astronomer Galileo when he used the newly invented telescope to look at the planets. The red world is called Io, and the white one Europa. A light one and a dark one—Ganymede and Callisto—will come into view in a minute. These four worlds, roughly the size of Earth's moon, are but four of Jupiter's *fifteen* moons.

Since the other eleven moons are only the size of asteroids, we'll pay attention to just these four—named the "Galilean satellites" in honor of Galileo. Being moons means that they circle around a much larger world. At the bottom of the page is a diagram of their orbits around Jupiter. It shows the path of *Voyager 1* through this system with the positions of the moons as it flies through. You can see that Voyager is going to get a very close look. Galileo would be envious. Will these moons he discovered be gaseous like Jupiter? This doesn't seem likely if they're as small as Earth's moon; they wouldn't have enough gravity to hold on to gases. Could they be rocky worlds like the Moon itself? We shall see. But as the diagram shows, we will pass Jupiter first—and it's going to be quite a show.

(Opposite) *Jupiter and two of its moons—both about the size of Earth's moon. (Compare with the photo of the Earth-Moon system on page 81.)*

◀

▼
Voyager 1's route past Jupiter and its moons.

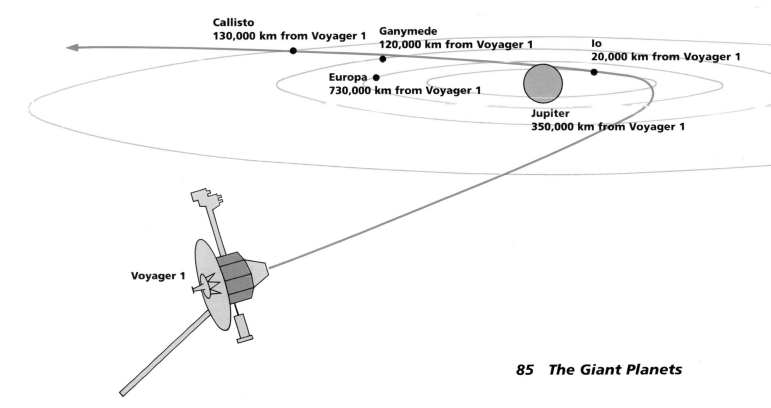

Callisto
130,000 km from Voyager 1

Ganymede
120,000 km from Voyager 1

Io
20,000 km from Voyager 1

Europa ●
730,000 km from Voyager 1

Jupiter
350,000 km from Voyager 1

Voyager 1

Closing in on Jupiter, we see that the giant planet looks like modern art. It's the biggest "painting" in the solar system! And what is the "paint" made of? Clouds—in many colors and layers. Scientists have discovered that the clouds are composed of hydrogen, helium, and complex molecules like ammonia and ammonium hydrosulfide. The red clouds are highest; next come the white clouds; then brown; and last of all, blue.

▼

The turbulent atmosphere of Jupiter.

Below that is an ocean of liquid hydrogen and helium, extending almost to the center of the planet. Jupiter almost certainly has no solid surface to stand, or land, on.

It may seem that Jupiter has a most unusual atmosphere, but it has one feature that should look familiar. The enormous red spot in the bottom left photograph is called, appropriately enough, the "Great Red Spot." Have you seen anything like it before? Think back to our Shuttle tour of planet Earth, when we saw a similar scene over the Gulf of Mexico—it is pictured at the bottom right.

Both features are giant storms. Earth's hurricane is 800 km (500 miles) wide. Jupiter's Red Spot—a violent storm that has been raging for at least three hundred years—is 40,000 km (25,000 miles) wide. Earth would sink like a basketball into those swirling red clouds. Pity to any sailors caught in the Spot on Jupiter's hydrogen seas.

Ever since we left the asteroid belt, Voyager has been under the influence of Jupiter's powerful gravity. We have been falling faster and faster toward the giant planet. By careful aiming we just miss it. And as we do so, our trajectory bends around the planet like a speedboat going around a buoy. Our new path sends us flying toward the four mysterious moons.

▼
Jupiter's largest storm (left), and Earth's largest storm (below). If Earth's hurricane were shown at the same scale as the Red Spot, it would be about as big as a BB.

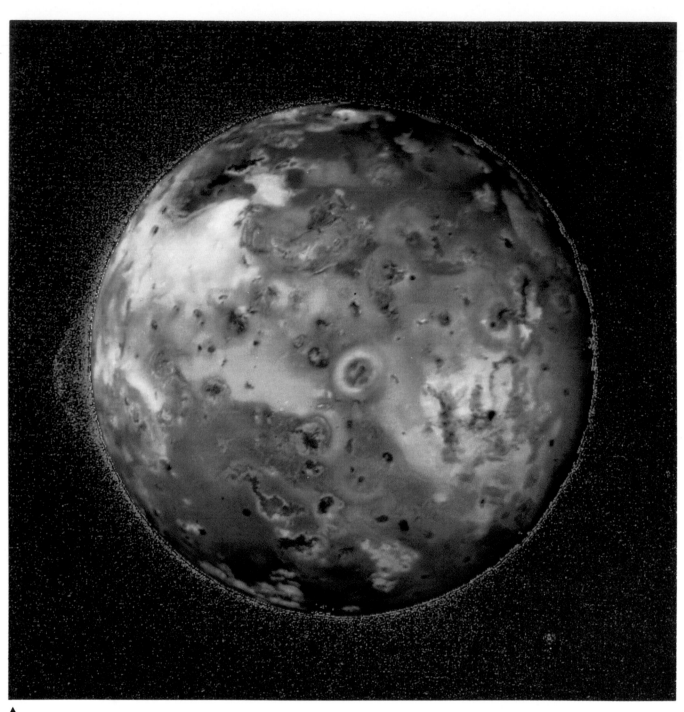

▲

Io—perhaps the most peculiar-looking object in the solar system . . .

First is Io. Like Mars, it appears reddish. And like Mars, it holds some surprises for us . . .

As one of the Voyager scientists says, "I've seen better-looking pizzas." Io is too small to have an atmosphere, so we are looking right down at the surface. Yet there are no craters. As we learned in the last chapter, this means that some weath-

▲

. . . and here's the reason. Io has volcanoes in almost continuous eruption, spreading an ever-changing coat of lava across the surface.

ering process is at work erasing them. But what could this process be if there is no atmosphere? Scientists are really puzzled by this until they do some computer processing on the pictures.

The picture above shows what they find.

Not only is this a volcano, but it's erupting. The closer scientists look, the more of these active volcanoes they discover.

There are nine in all. Clearly, this is the process that is "weathering" Io's surface—and we see it happening before our very eyes. When scientists ask themselves what is pouring out of those volcanoes, no one is sure. Some think molten sulfur. Others think it is Earthlike lava. But everyone agrees that this is one of the most exciting discoveries of the space age. Active volcanoes have never before been seen beyond Earth. And here is a world where they are in almost constant eruption!

Unfortunately, there's no slowing down for a longer look. At 30 km/sec (20 miles/sec) Voyager is already saying good-bye to Io and training its cameras on Jupiter's next moon, Europa.

. . . And then, just as quickly, we are off to Ganymede.

Europa (top), and Ganymede (bottom) are also unlike any worlds we have yet seen. To the right are close-ups of Europa's intricate cracks and Ganymede's grooved bands.

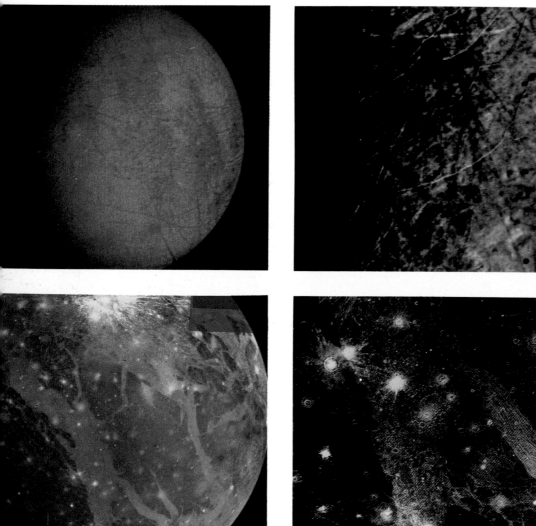

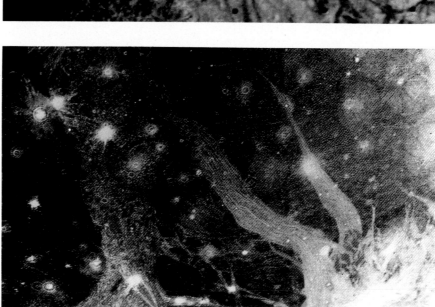

. . . And finally, Callisto.

Each of these moons differs from the others. Europa has an unbelievably smooth surface broken by millions of intersecting lines, like a cracked billiard ball. Ganymede resembles Earth's moon — until close inspection shows a strange and complicated system of grooves crisscrossing the world like freeways. Callisto is as packed with craters as a world can possibly be. All three are ice-coated worlds; their lithospheres are ordinary frozen water.

The solar system truly gets stranger and stranger as we get farther and farther from Earth. What could be next? For months on end there will be nothing. We will sail through utter

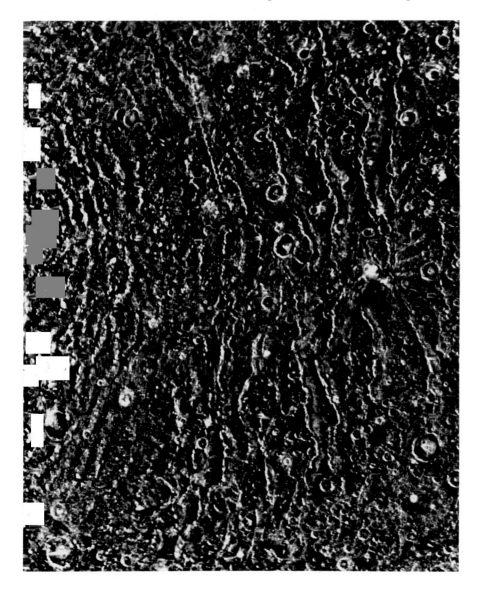

Last of the Galliloan satollitoc, Callisto has a huge impact feature like the ones on the Moon and Mercury (see page 55). But instead of being formed in rock, the circular basin is made of solid ice. The close-up at left shows the frozen "ripples" from this giant splash, radiating from the left edge of the picture.

blackness with nothing but faraway stars to look at. But then, like a lonely island on the sea, the most mysterious of all the planets will come into view.

This planet needs no introduction. It's everyone's idea of how a planet should look—an enormous sphere surrounded by a broad, flat ring. It's Saturn. Saturn is only slightly smaller than Jupiter and about one-third as massive. Like Jupiter, it consists almost entirely of hydrogen and helium gas.

Saturn's rings have been a puzzle since they were discovered in the 1600s. The first maps that showed this curious feature included the reassurance, "Saturn really does look like this—we're not kidding." In those days everyone thought the rings were a giant plate. Much later, scientists realized that this was not possible because the rings were actually *orbiting* Saturn. According to the laws of orbital motion, the inside of the plate would move faster than the outside, and the plate would be

Ring Around Jupiter

As if Voyager were not already sending back enough surprises, something really unexpected turned up in the empty space near Jupiter: a ring! In this photograph, Jupiter's ring is seen from the planet's night side, stretching to the right and left like a miniature version of Saturn's rings.

For comparison, Saturn's ring system is 74,000 km (46,000 miles) wide and shows up easily in a small telescope from Earth. The portion of Jupiter's ring visible here is less than 1,000 km (600 miles) across. The ring is so thin that it blocks only a millionth of the light passing through, making it ten thousand times more transparent than glass.

What is it made of? Scientists are not sure, but they believe it is composed of tiny particles ejected from volcanoes on the nearby moon Io.

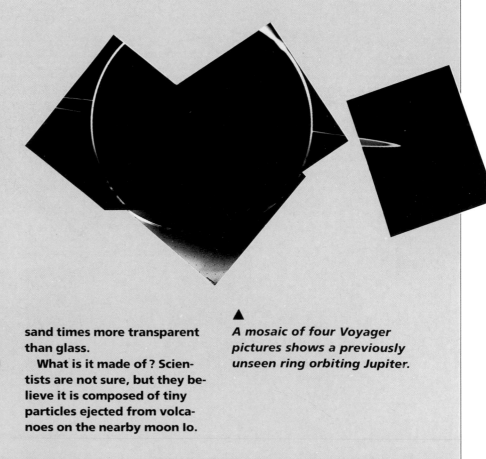

▲
A mosaic of four Voyager pictures shows a previously unseen ring orbiting Jupiter.

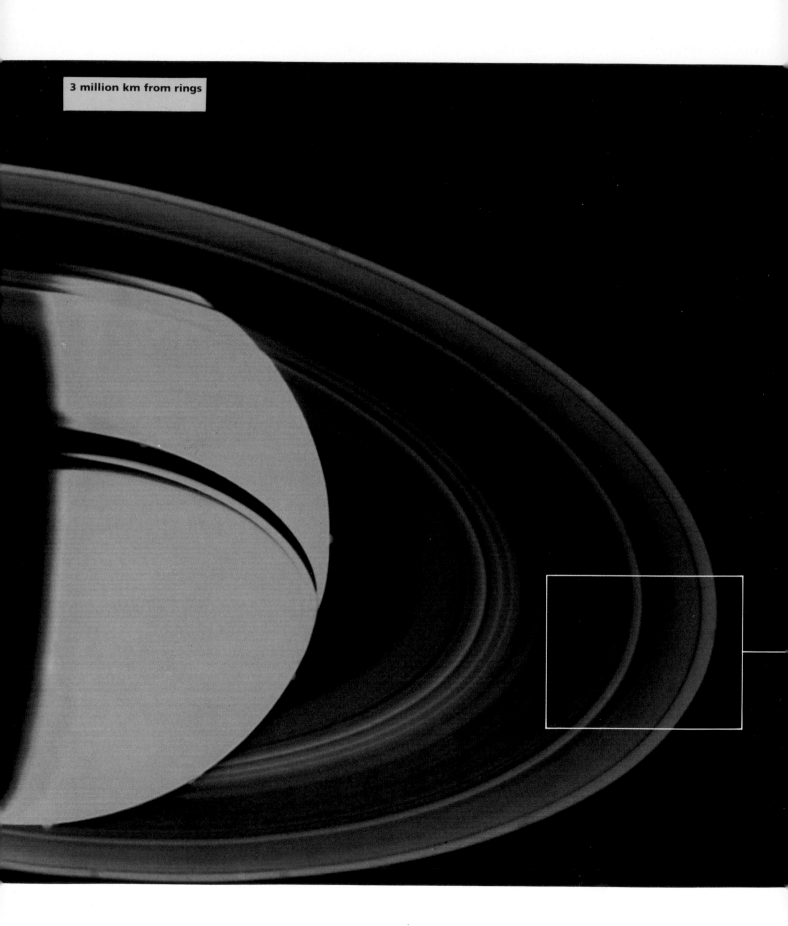

ripped apart. So scientists concluded that the rings must be composed of many particles orbiting independently.

How big are the particles? What are they made of? How are they organized? It is Voyager's mission to find out.

Scientists back home are astounded when they see the pictures sent back by Voyager. Where they had expected perhaps a dozen divisions in the rings, they see tens of thousands. The ring system looks like a giant phonograph record.

Voyager is too far away to photograph individual ring particles. But there are other methods. Do you recall how *Mariner 10's* radio signal was used to measure the thickness of Venus's atmosphere? Voyager uses a similar trick. As its radio beams through the rings, the signal is interrupted by the ring particles and their size can be determined. Most particles prove to be about as big as beach balls. Some are as large as houses, and many are probably no more than dust specks. Other instruments show that the particles consist of ordinary water ice.

Where did the rings come from? Voyager doesn't answer this question, but scientists believe one clue may be Saturn's moons. There are twenty-one of them and almost all of them are composed of solid ice. Could one of these ice moons have ventured too close to Saturn and broken apart, leaving a ring

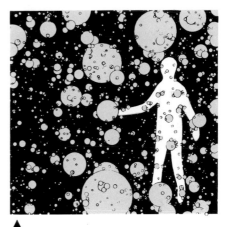

▲
A computer reconstruction of the particles in a room-size section of Saturn's rings. A silhouetted Earthling is shown for scale.

740,000 km from rings

50,000 km from rings

A visitor approaching Saturn would find that its broad, flat ring system is composed of thousands of small ringlets and that the ringlets are made up of countless particles of ice.

Picture Puzzle

Voyager's cameras convert a picture into nearly a million individual spots of light called *pixels* (short for "picture elements"). The brightness of each pixel is then converted into a number. Why a number?

Think of a photograph as being composed of many columns of numbers. Each number represents a shade of gray, from white to black. You can "send" such a picture over the phone simply by reading the list of numbers. The person at the other end converts the numbers into the corresponding gray levels, and *presto* — a picture! (A color picture is made up of three such images, as explained at left.) Voyager transmits photographs to Earth in exactly this way, only the numbers are further simplified into a series of on/off radio pulses called digital signals that are easier to send over long distances.

On Earth the whole process is reversed: digital signals to numbers; numbers to gray levels; and *presto* — a picture!

Voyager takes color pictures by shooting a scene three times through blue, green, and red filters. When each scene is printed in the corresponding color, full-color appears where the scenes overlap, as above. The principle is that of additive color: blue, green, and red lights can be combined to produce all colors.

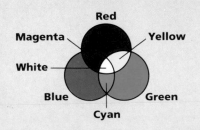

1
Voyager takes picture

2
Picture converted into numbers and radioed to Earth

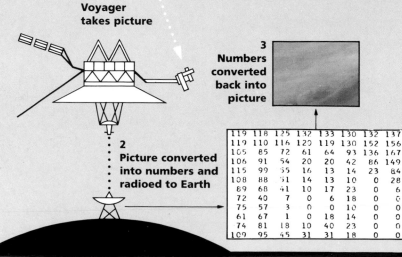

3
Numbers converted back into picture

119	118	125	132	133	130	132	137
119	110	116	120	119	130	152	156
105	85	72	61	64	93	136	167
106	91	54	20	20	42	86	149
115	99	55	16	13	14	23	84
108	88	51	14	13	10	0	28
89	68	41	10	17	23	0	6
72	40	7	0	6	18	0	0
75	57	3	0	0	10	0	0
61	67	1	0	18	14	0	0
74	81	18	10	40	23	0	0
109	95	45	31	31	18	0	0

Red

Magenta — Yellow

White

Blue — Green

Cyan

of frosty debris? Another theory is that, like the asteroids, the rings are building blocks for a world that never formed.

And what of these twenty-one moons? Below are a few of them.

One is Mimas, which was nearly torn apart by a meteor the size of Mount Everest. The crater from that explosion—four billion years ago—dominates the landscape.

Another is Iapetus, a two-toned world partly coated in a mysterious black substance. What is it? No one knows.

The moon Hyperion looks like a hamburger.

And on orange-colored Titan, the absence of surface detail is a clue that we're seeing something *really* interesting—an atmosphere.

Titan is Saturn's largest moon. It is larger than the planet Mercury, and its atmosphere is denser than Earth's. The clouds on Titan are methane—the same gas we use in gas stoves. We can't see through the clouds but some scientists speculate that on Titan's surface, waves from liquid methane seas wash against continents of solid ice, and the temperature is a chilly −180 degrees C (−290 degrees Fahrenheit). Others agree that it's cold, but think that Titan's oceans are really liquid ethane (a chemical similar to methane), and that a strange acetylene snow falls from the sky and settles to the bottom of the cold, cold seas. The solar system really does get stranger and stranger.

Jupiter, Io, Europa, Ganymede, Callisto, Saturn, Mimas, Iapetus, Hyperion, Titan—all are totally unlike anything in Earth's neighborhood. None of these worlds could have formed in the inner solar system. Imagine what would happen if you took one of these ice moons to the orbit of Mercury. It would melt.

Along the bottom: Mimas, Iapetus, and Hyperion. These tiny moons of Saturn were discovered in 1789, 1671, and 1848 respectively. Yet no one knew what they looked like until 1980–81, when Voyagers 1 and 2 took these pictures. Saturn's largest moon, Titan (directly below), was discovered in 1655, and we still don't know how it looks. Orange clouds completely shroud Titan, and scientists would like to send a radar spacecraft to map its surface.
▼

Titan

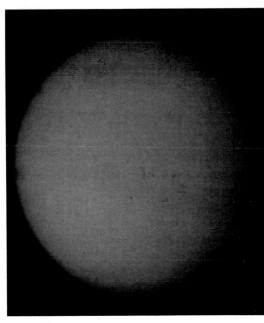

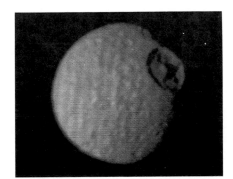

Mimas

Iapetus

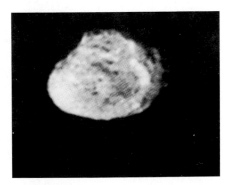

Hyperion

The Sun sets the rules in the solar system. Not only does it govern the conditions on the planets, but it determines which planets go where: small rocky worlds in the inner solar system, gaseous giants and ice worlds in the outer solar system. These rules don't explain the origin of the planets, but scientists think the Sun had a lot to do with that, too.

Billions of years ago, when the Sun was beginning to form from an enormous cloud of dust and gas, a small part of the material spun off to produce the planets. And around the larger of these planets, excess material went into the creation of moons. All of the evidence from spacecraft supports this picture of our origins. As we saw earlier, the light gases were pushed by the Sun's heat into the outer solar system. In Earth's vicinity only the heavier, rocky materials remained—the building blocks for the firm ground beneath us.

Voyager 1 emerges from behind Saturn on a northerly course taking it out of the solar system. The next object it passes will be a star near the Little Dipper in the year 42318 A.D., over 40,000 years from now. Fortunately for us, *Voyager 2's* next encounter is a little sooner, so we will stay aboard it for now. On January 24, 1986, *Voyager 2* will pass Uranus, the next planet beyond Saturn. Three years and seven months later, it will complete its mission when it flies within 7,500 km (4,700 miles) of Neptune, at the outer limits of the solar system.

What will we find at Uranus and Neptune? Until 1986 and 1989 arrive, we can only speculate based on what little we know from telescopic observations.

Your guess is as good as anybody's. Remember that when the Voyagers left Earth for Jupiter and Saturn, no one dreamed of the astonishing discoveries they would make. Surely Uranus

Saturn's mass = 95 times Earth's mass

Uranus's mass = 15 times Earth's mass

and Neptune are saving a few surprises, too. Perhaps you can guess what they might be.

Will the atmospheres be as colorful as Jupiter's?

What will the dark rings at Uranus be?

Will Neptune have rings?

What about the moons? Will we discover strange new features? — liquid nitrogen oceans? — methane volcanoes?

Who knows? Be sure and stay tuned in the months ahead.

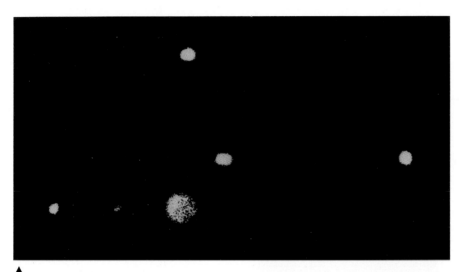

▲
A telescopic view of Uranus and its five known moons. In 1977 a special technique discovered rings around Uranus. They can't be seen here, but Voyager 2 should tell us more about them in 1986.

▶
Our best view of Neptune, showing high altitude clouds of ice crystals. Will Neptune turn out to have rings like the other giant planets?

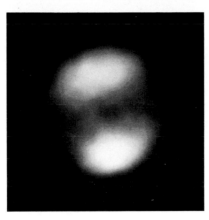

Neptune's mass =
17 times
Earth's mass

Uranus

- **Position:**
  Seventh planet from Sun

- **Distance from Sun:**
  3 billion km
  (2 billion miles)

- **Length of year:**
  84 Earth years

- **Length of day:**
  11 hours

- **Diameter:**
  52,000 km (32,000 miles
  — 4 times Earth's diameter)

Uranus is bluish green, with an atmosphere that is probably hydrogen, helium, and methane. At least five moons orbit Uranus, as well as a system of nine very dark and very thin rings.

Neptune

- **Position:**
  Eighth planet from Sun

- **Distance from Sun:**
  4.5 billion km
  (3 billion miles)

- **Length of year:**
  165 Earth years

- **Length of day:**
  18 hours

- **Diameter:**
  50,000 km (31,000 miles
  — 4 times Earth's diameter)

Neptune has a greenish color, two moons, and an atmosphere similar to Uranus's. Little else is known.

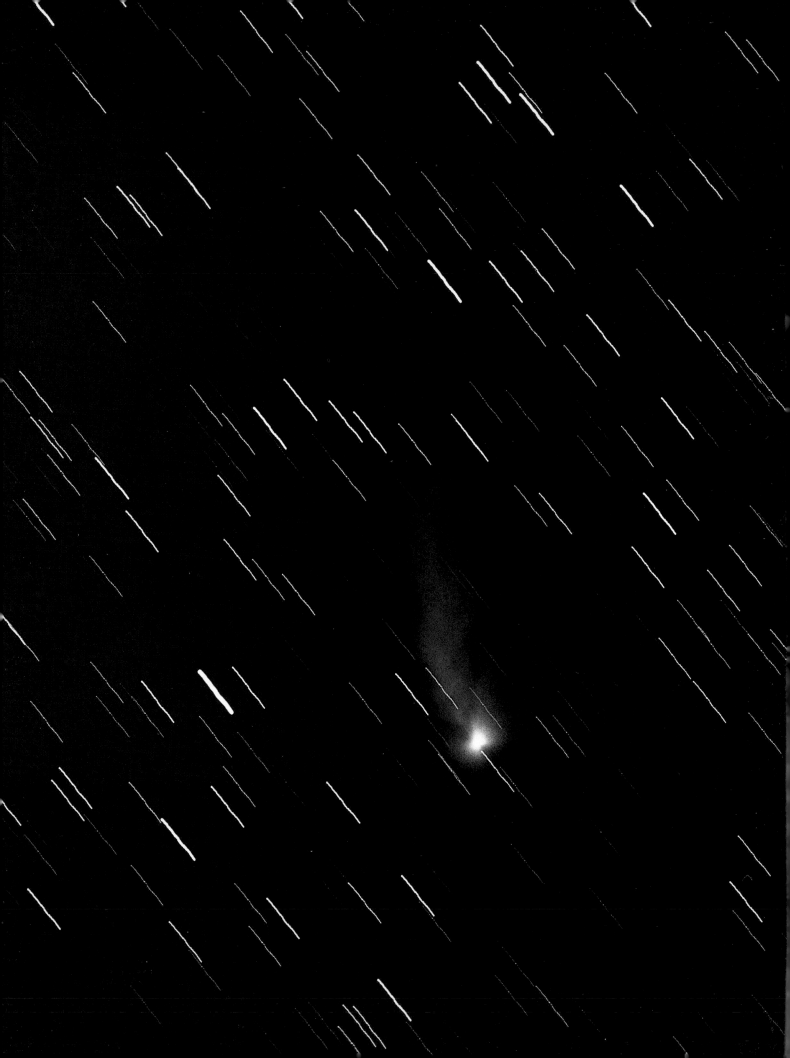

Chapter 8

Pluto and Beyond

We certainly have come a long way since we climbed aboard the Shuttle back in Chapter 1. Then it seemed like a big step just to leave Earth and go into orbit. Now we are exploring deepest, darkest space, at the far reaches of the solar system. After passing Neptune, *Voyager 2* will sail on. In 1990 it will cross the path of Pluto, the outermost known planet. But Pluto will not be there. It will be elsewhere in its orbit, billions of kilometers away. We must wait for some future spaceship to fly close by and show us this remote world. Until then, the indistinct views below are about all we will be able to see.

In these photographs through a powerful telescope, Pluto shows up as a tiny, blurry point of light. Actually, the blur includes both Pluto *and* its moon, Charon, orbiting 17,000 km (11,000 miles) out from Pluto's surface. Telescopes on Earth are too distant to see the space between these two worlds, and so they appear as a single object.

(Opposite) *A hazy comet traverses space between Jupiter and the asteroid belt on its journey from beyond Pluto. The far distant stars appear as streaks — like blurred spectators in a race car picture — because the telescope is following the comet's motion.*
◀

(Bottom left) *Pluto against a background of stars that includes a galaxy in the lower right-hand corner (we will soon see more of these). (Right) Pluto in a close-up showing the bulge that proved to be a moon. The drawing over the photo shows the true size of Pluto and its moon.*
▼

Halley's Comet

Far beyond Pluto, a third of the way to the nearest star, several billion chunks of ice and dust circle the Sun in long, lazy orbits. This region is the storehouse for the solar system's comets. Occasionally, a passing star will give a gravitational nudge to some of this debris, sending it falling toward the Sun.

After a few million years, these "dirty snowballs" enter the inner solar system and begin to look more familiar. Their surface layers of ice vaporize from the Sun's intense heat, streaming backward into space to form a long tail. The tail gets longer and longer as a comet gets closer to the Sun.

Few comets actually hit the Sun. Most swing around it and head back into deep space on very elongated orbits. They will not be seen again for millions of years, if ever. But occasionally a comet will pass close to Jupiter or Saturn and have its orbit bent by the planet's powerful gravity. These comets become trapped within the region of the planets, returning to the Sun at frequent intervals.

The most famous of these frequent visitors is named for Edmund Halley, a friend of Isaac Newton. In 1705 Halley was calculating orbits for different comets and noticed something similar about those observed in 1531, 1607, and 1682. He decided that they were, in fact, the same comet coming back at about seventy-six-year intervals. Halley predicted that this comet would be observed again around 1758. When it appeared on schedule, it was named in his honor.

Records of Halley's Comet reach back to 240 B.C. — about the time an obscure city called Rome conquered all of Italy. Halley's Comet has been around the Sun twenty-seven times since then, and is next expected in 1985–1986. In the late fall of 1985, the comet will appear in the constellation Taurus as it passes within 90 million km (60 million miles) of Earth. Watch for it— you may need binoculars.

In case you miss it, spaceships are being sent from Europe, Japan, and Russia to fly close to Halley's Comet in the spring of 1986. They should provide fascinating information on this mysterious visitor from beyond Pluto.

▼

(Top) *Halley's Comet during its last passage in 1910 and* (bottom) *in the Bayeux Tapestry as an omen of the 1066 invasion of England by William the Conqueror.*

What is Pluto like? No one is sure, but one clue is its peculiar orbit around the Sun.

For twenty years out of every 248, Pluto's orbit carries it inside the orbit of Neptune, making Neptune temporarily the farthest planet. We happen to be living at such a moment now; it will last until 1999, when Pluto will sail beyond Neptune and regain its title. This peculiar path—weaving in and then out of Neptune's orbit—causes some scientists to think that Pluto may be an escaped moon of Neptune's. Pluto certainly has the properties of a moon. It is even smaller than Earth's moon, and it probably consists of solid ice. Could Pluto be like the ice moons orbiting Saturn? Maybe so, but with a chilling difference: those worlds are made of water ice; Pluto is almost certainly frozen methane gas at a temperature of −215 degrees C (−419 degrees Fahrenheit).

In 1805 Lewis and Clark stood on the shores of western North America and looked out across the vast Pacific Ocean. They had traveled overland across an entire continent, and they could go no further. In the twenty-first century perhaps astronauts will stand on the frozen surface of Pluto and look out across the heavens. They, too, will have reached a limit. Behind them will be the planets. Ahead will be the gulf of space—a vast emptiness leading to the stars.

Will the spacefarers of the future be able to travel to the stars? Let's hope so. We know that it is impossible today. The nearest star to our solar system is 40 *trillion* km (25 trillion miles) away. (A trillion is a million million.) It would take many thousands of years to get there using the most powerful rockets in existence. Until we can discover the secret of interstellar travel, Pluto will be the end of the line.

But *Voyager 2* sails on—a slow boat to the stars. In 44,426 years it will pass within 10 trillion km (6 trillion miles) of the obscure star AC+79 3888. This will be just the first of many encounters stretching out over billions of years. We would be wise, however, to leave Voyager and continue our explorations from the comforts of Earth.

On a clear night, on a high mountain, and looking through a powerful telescope, we can see wonders in the starry sky over our home planet.

Pluto

- *Position:*
  Ninth planet from the Sun

- *Distance from Sun:*
  **6 billion km
  (4 billion miles)**

- *Length of year:*
  248 Earth years

- *Length of day:*
  6 Earth days

- *Diameter:*
  **2,500 km (1,500 miles—
  ⅕ Earth's diameter)**

Since a year on Pluto is 248 Earth years, the most distant planet has not even had time to complete a single orbit of the Sun since its discovery in 1930. That first full Pluto year will end in our year 2178—about two centuries from now.

Earth

Pluto

It is a magnificent view. And just as the planets show surprising differences, so do the stars. We can see all sizes, kinds, and colors. How do we understand such variety, especially if we can't travel out to the stars and look at them from close up?

Actually, there is one star that we *can* see from close up. We have been in its company for our entire voyage. We have watched it growing dimmer and dimmer until, at the edge of the solar system, it is just a bright star among millions of stars. It is the Sun.

This is the great fire that has lit our way among the planets. It is the enormous burning sphere that bakes the surface of Mercury, and it is the tiny beacon in the cold sky over Pluto. On Earth, animals and plants depend on it no less than on food and water. Indeed, food would not grow and water would freeze without the Sun.

What do we know about it? How does it work? How big is it? Will it last forever? The answers to these questions tell not only the story of our Sun, but the story of all the stars.

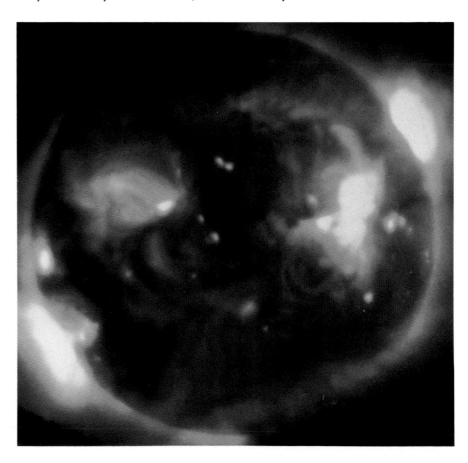

▶

While the Sun may seem just plain bright to us, an x-ray picture like this one shows that certain parts of it burn hotter than others. The hot spots are gigantic storms of superheated gases. At this scale the Earth is about twice the size of the period at the end of this sentence.

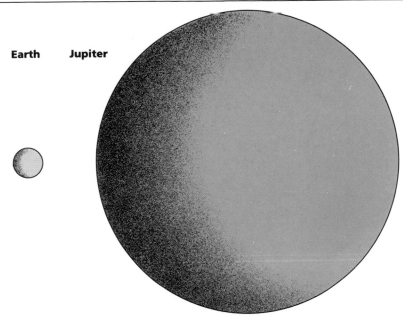

Earth   Jupiter   Sun

As you can see in the drawing, the Sun is too big to fit on the page at the same scale as Earth and Jupiter. If we represented the Sun with a large yellow beach ball, Earth would be the size of a pea, orbiting 60 meters (200 feet, or two-thirds of a football field) away, and Jupiter would be the size of a tennis ball 300 meters (1,000 feet) away. Like Jupiter, the Sun is composed mainly of hydrogen and helium gas.

Needless to say, the Sun is hot. At its very center the temperature is 16 million degrees C (29 million degrees Fahrenheit). This is hot enough to break the bonds of ordinary matter, fusing atoms of hydrogen into helium and releasing huge explosions of energy. This same reaction takes place when a hydrogen bomb is set off. The fusion reaction in a hydrogen bomb lasts a millionth of a second. But the Sun has been exploding for five billion years.

What caused the Sun to start burning in the first place? The answer lies in its tremendous mass. More mass means more pressure pushing down on the center of an object, and more pressure means higher temperatures. Any celestial body that is about seventy times more massive than Jupiter—or about seven percent of the Sun's mass—will be hot enough to start fusion reactions at its very center. Such an object will become a star. This is why Jupiter and the Sun can be made of the same materials, yet one is a star and the other isn't. Mass determines whether a world will be a rocky asteroid, a planet with an atmosphere, or a giant star, burning for billions of years.

According to some astronomers, this donut-shaped cloud is material being thrown off by the star at the very center, which is collapsing into a white dwarf.

If it's one huge hydrogen bomb, then why doesn't the Sun blow itself to bits? Again, the reason is its enormous mass. The Sun weighs almost a thousand times more than all of the rest of the solar system combined—planets, moons, asteroids, everything. Indeed, the Sun not only holds itself together, but it holds the solar system together. Its tremendous gravity tugs at the planets and keeps them in their orbits.

Will the Sun ever burn out? It will, but don't panic. The Sun has enough hydrogen fuel to keep its fusion fires burning for another five billion years. Then a very curious thing will happen. Hydrogen will run out in the hot core, and the Sun will start burning the "ashes" that are left over—helium, carbon, neon, oxygen, and silicon. At the same time the Sun will also start to expand, turning red as its swelling surface cools. In a short time it will swell out to the orbit of Mercury. Then its red fires will engulf Venus. And then . . .

On Earth it won't be too pleasant. The oceans will turn to steam; the continents will melt; and finally, the planet will vaporize. All that will remain of Earth will be a few pieces of rock and some scraps of metal that, long before, were fashioned into spaceships like Voyager and sent out to the stars. Voyager will probably outlast the planet that created it.

The Sun's expansion will eventually stop and it will shine as a *red giant* for a few million years, until its fuels are exhausted. Then the final collapse will begin. The once life-giving Sun will shrink to a glowing cinder about the size of the former planet Earth. It will become a supercompressed, used-up star called a *white dwarf.*

This is the life cycle of any star of about the Sun's size and mass: born from a cloud of interstellar gas; blazing in the peak of health for a few billion years; bloating into a red giant; and collapsing into a pale and exhausted white dwarf. So it goes.

But while our Sun may seem big and important to us, it is really just an average-sized star with an average life history. More massive stars have far more spectacular careers. Stars heavier than the Sun burn hotter and brighter, but for a shorter time. They are the gas guzzlers of the cosmos. And any star that is more than four times heavier than the Sun will end its days not in the red giant phase, but by exploding in a flash of fire more brilliant than a billion Suns. This celestial firework is called a *supernova*.

On the night of July 4, 1054, Chinese astronomers observed a brilliant light where they had seen no star before. They called it a "guest star" and watched closely as it slowly disappeared over the course of a year. What they had seen was a distant supernova explosion. Today, nine hundred years later, if we aim a telescope at the dark patch of sky where the Chinese saw their "guest star," this is what we find.

▼

The Crab Nebula—a celestial firecracker that exploded on July Fourth over nine hundred years ago.

Don Dixon painted this hypothetical view of a black hole sucking in matter from a nearby star. The black hole is, of course, invisible, but it reveals its presence by the emissions from the superheated gases spiraling into it.

The explosion is still visible. In nine hundred years it has expanded from perhaps a few times the Sun's diameter to *ten thousand times* the diameter of the solar system. Only recently astronomers observed a strange new kind of star at the center of the exploding cloud. This object is about 10 km (6 miles) across, yet it is as heavy as the Sun. And it spins at the extraordinary rate of thirty times a second, beaming out rapid pulses of energy like a celestial lighthouse. This pulsing, superdense star is called a *pulsar*.

Pulsars, supernovas, white dwarfs and red giants. Science truth really is stranger than science fiction. But the strangest thing in the universe is a star that doesn't shine. It is denser than a white dwarf—denser even than a pulsar. And its gravitational field overpowers everything in its vicinity. You have no doubt heard of it. It is called a *black hole*.

Imagine a normal-sized vacuum cleaner so powerful that it sucks up the dirt, the carpet, the floor, the house, the continents and the oceans—in fact the whole Earth! But it doesn't stop there. This vacuum cleaner packs in the Moon, Venus, Mercury, Mars . . . all of the moons and planets—everything we studied through Chapter 7—into a normal vacuum cleaner bag. We would then have something that approximates the density—the compactness—of a black hole. Indeed, we could now turn off the vacuum motor (assuming the motor was doing all of this) because now the black hole would suck in almost everything within millions of kilometers on its own. The gravitational field surrounding a black hole is so strong that not even *light* can escape. How do we see it? We can't. It is literally a "black hole" in space.

Astronomers believe that many stars larger than the Sun collapse into black holes once their stellar fires die out. But if we can't see black holes, how do we know where they are? Well, we look for unusual events happening for no apparent reason: a whirlpool of matter being sucked into nowhere; a massive star orbiting an empty point in space; the bending of starlight around an invisible object. Watch out for anything peculiar—it may be a black hole.

We are now nearing the end of our journey. We have covered quite a lot of territory in these eight chapters. We have

Good Neighbors

The stars are so far away that the closest ones are still featureless points of light, even when viewed through a powerful telescope. The dazzling star at the top of this picture is Alpha Centauri, the second-closest star to our solar system. The photograph has been greatly overexposed so that we can make out the actual *closest* star, Proxima Centauri, indicated at the bottom. Both are about 40 trillion km (give or take a few hundred billion) from Earth. Yet they are our nearest neighbors in our tiny out-of-the-way section of the Milky Way Galaxy.

Why does Proxima look so insignificant compared with Alpha? Astronomers believe that Proxima is only one-twentieth the diameter of the Sun, which makes it smaller than Jupiter. If Proxima Centauri were at the same dis-

tance as the Sun, it would shine with about as much light as forty-five full Moons. This may seem bright, but the Sun is *ten thousand* times brighter. Alpha Centauri is also about ten thousand times brighter, meaning that it is a star very much like our Sun.

▲
At the top is our close neighbor Alpha Centauri, a star much like our Sun—and perhaps a sun for its own collection of planets. Proxima Centauri, the closest star to us, is at the lower left.

orbited Earth in the Space Shuttle; we have flown to the Moon with Apollo; we have ventured to the planets aboard *Mariner 10,* Viking, and Voyager.

We have seen that conditions on the planets are governed by their size and their closeness to the Sun—that we only find life where the temperature is not too hot, not too cold, and the planet is neither too small nor too large. We have found one such perfect planet: Earth.

From Pluto we have seen the Sun as merely a bright star among millions of stars. We have learned how the Sun and the other stars live, and the bizarre ways in which they die.

There is almost nothing in the great and glorious sky that we have not explored by spaceship or by telescope. *Almost nothing . . .*

▶

When seen with the unaided eye, the Andromeda Galaxy is a faint smudge of light (the drawing on the opposite page shows how to find it). Here we see it through a large telescope, showing that Andromeda is really made up of billions of stars.

▼

Also made up of billions of stars is our own Milky Way, a galaxy very much like Andromeda, and the one in which we happen to live. This map is compiled from hundreds of photographs of the night sky and shows an insider's view of our galaxy. Andromeda, the closest galaxy to us, is faintly visible at the lower left.

Sometime when you're out in the country, far away from city lights, look for a prominent group of stars called "Cassiopeia's Chair." In autumn these stars are high in the midnight sky over Earth's northern hemisphere. They look like a big *M* or *W*, and the ancient Greeks imagined they were the throne of the mythical Queen Cassiopeia. Follow one of the points of the throne to a hazy patch of light, shown here.

To the Persians in the tenth century this barely visible smudge was known as the "Little Cloud." How does the Little Cloud look through a big telescope? (See opposite page.)

Some cloud. When astronomers in the nineteenth century turned their telescopes on this sight, some of them were convinced that they had discovered an "island universe" — another universe of stars, unimaginably distant. They compared it in size with the broad band of stars that crosses the sky, called the "Milky Way."

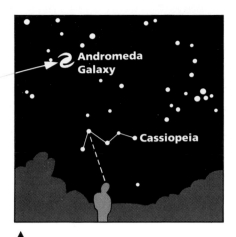

▲
The Andromeda Galaxy, known as the "Little Cloud" in ancient times, can be found with the aid of the "pointer" stars in Cassiopeia. Choose a very dark night and bring along binoculars.

▲
A group of five galaxies at a distance of three hundred million light years. Light rays from these galaxies travel across space at 300,000 km/sec (186,000 miles/sec) for three hundred million years before reaching Earth.

▶
(Opposite) Three of the estimated one hundred billion galaxies in our universe. Do any of them have stars, circled by planets, populated by intelligent life that is looking back at us?

At the time, it was thought that the Milky Way was all that there was to the universe. This was quite enough for most people, since the Milky Way is really a vast system of perhaps 500 billion stars, including our Sun and every other star visible with the unaided eye.

The Milky Way forms a huge disk about a billion billion kilometers in diameter. This is 25,000 times the distance to the nearest star, or *100 million* times the diameter of the solar system. A beam of light, traveling at the phenomenal speed of 300,000 km/sec (186,000 miles/sec), takes 100,000 years to cross the Milky Way. How could there possibly be anything more?

But there is more. By now, we should not be surprised to find out that the universe is bigger than we supposed. It turns out there are many such islands. They are called *galaxies*. The Little Cloud near Cassiopeia is just the closest galaxy to our own—a mere two million years of light-travel time away.

Sweeping our giant telescopes across the sky, we can pick out an unbelievable number of galaxies—billions of them, each composed of billions of stars. How many of the stars have planets? How many of the planets are not too big, not too little, not too hot, not too cold, with water and an oxygen-rich atmosphere? How many have already sent out explorers to learn about the universe that we all share?

No one knows. As explorers from Space Station Earth, we have a big job ahead.

Index

Credits

We wish to thank the following NASA Installations for supplying the great majority of photographs used in this book: Johnson Space Center, Jet Propulsion Laboratory, National Space Science Data Center, Kennedy Space Center, Ames Research Center, and NASA Headquarters. Thanks also to Diane McCaffery and Mary Reilly who produced the drawings and to Chris Pullman who art directed.

Additional material was obtained courtesy of the following individuals, institutions, and publications:

2 (left) B. Gire, in *Spaceflight*, September/October 1982
5 (bottom) Smithsonian Institution, photo number B4-14155
13 (top left) Yerkes Observatory
13 (top right) from Newton's *The System of the World*, 1729
20 (top) Richard Frear/National Park Service
25 (right) EROS Data Center/NOAA
38 (left) U. S. Geological Survey
40–41 (top) Defense Mapping Agency Aerospace Center, St. Louis, Missouri
45 (top) Robert Victor, Abrams Planetarium, Michigan State University
47 (top) Robert Victor/Abrams Planetarium and James Seevers/Adler Planetarium
52 James Garvin, Maria Zuber, and Paul Helfenstein, Department of Geological Sciences, Brown University
53 Michael Kobrick/JPL
56 Lowell Observatory
57 from Schiaparelli's *Osservazioni*, 1881
59 (top) © 1939 by Ziff-Davis Publishing Co., reprinted by permission of Forrest J Ackerman, 2495 Glendower Ave., Hollywood, California 90027, for the Estate of Frank R. Paul
59 (bottom) Film Stills Archive/Museum of Modern Art

62 Lick Observatory
67 (inset) EROS Data Center/NOAA and Flagstaff Image Processing Facility/USGS
68 Paul Hudson
72 (top right) Lick Observatory
74 C. F. Capen/IPRO Planetary Library and Archive
75 Dan Haar/*Hartford Courant*
99 (top) W. M. Sinton, Institute for Astronomy, University of Hawaii
99 (bottom) Stephen Larson, Lunar and Planetary Laboratory, University of Arizona
100 © 1965 by California Institute of Technology and Carnegie Institution of Washington, reproduced by permission from Palomar Observatory, California Institute of Technology
101 (left) Lick Observatory
101 (right) U. S. Naval Observatory
102 (top) Mount Wilson and Las Campanas Observatories, Carnegie Institution of Washington
102 (bottom) Yerkes Observatory
104–105 Royal Observatory, Edinburgh
108 Lick Observatory
109 Palomar Observatory, California Institute of Technology
110 Don Dixon
111 Harvard College Observatory
112 (top) Palomar Observatory, California Institute of Technology
112–113 (bottom) Lund Observatory, Sweden
114 Lick Observatory
115 (all) Palomar Observatory, California Institute of Technology

The NOVA television series is made possible by funding from public television stations, and by grants from Allied Corporation, and the Johnson & Johnson Family of Companies.